I0042522

Standards for the Control of Algorithmic Bias

The Canadian Administrative Context

Governments around the world use machine learning in automated decision-making systems for a broad range of functions. However, algorithmic bias in machine learning can result in automated decisions that produce disparate impact and may compromise *Charter* guarantees of substantive equality. This book seeks to answer the question: what standards should be applied to machine learning to mitigate disparate impact in government use of automated decision-making?

The regulatory landscape for automated decision-making, in Canada and across the world, is far from settled. Legislative and policy models are emerging, and the role of standards is evolving to support regulatory objectives. While acknowledging the contributions of leading standards development organizations, the authors argue that the rationale for standards must come from the law and that implementing such standards would help to reduce future complaints *by*, and would proactively enable human rights protections *for*, those subject to automated decision-making. The book presents a proposed standards framework for automated decision-making and provides recommendations for its implementation in the context of the government of Canada's Directive on Automated Decision-Making.

As such, this book can assist public agencies around the world in developing and deploying automated decision-making systems equitably as well as being of interest to businesses that utilize automated decision-making processes.

Natalie Heisler has advised public- and private-sector organizations around the world in the strategy and deployment of data, analytics, and artificial intelligence for more than 20 years. Natalie brings a unique, multidisciplinary perspective to her work, spanning social, regulatory, policy, and technical dimensions. Natalie has a BA in Psychology, an MSc in Mathematics, and an MA in Political Science and lives in Toronto, Canada.

Maura R. Grossman, JD, PhD, is a research professor in the David R. Cheriton School of Computer Science at the University of Waterloo and an affiliate faculty member at the Vector Institute of Artificial Intelligence, both in Ontario, Canada. She also is the principal at Maura Grossman Law, in Buffalo, New York, USA. Professor Grossman's multidisciplinary work falls at the intersection of law, health, technology, ethics, and policy.

Standards for the Control of Algorithmic Bias
The Canadian Administrative Context

Natalie Heisler
and
Maura R. Grossman

CRC Press
Taylor & Francis Group
Boca Raton London New York

CRC Press is an imprint of the
Taylor & Francis Group, an **informa** business

First edition published 2024
by CRC Press
6000 Broken Sound Parkway NW, Suite 300, Boca Raton, FL 33487-2742

and by CRC Press
4 Park Square, Milton Park, Abingdon, Oxon, OX14 4RN

© 2024 Natalie Heisler & Maura R. Grossman

Reasonable efforts have been made to publish reliable data and information, but the author and publisher cannot assume responsibility for the validity of all materials or the consequences of their use. The authors and publishers have attempted to trace the copyright holders of all material reproduced in this publication and apologize to copyright holders if permission to publish in this form has not been obtained. If any copyright material has not been acknowledged please write and let us know so we may rectify in any future reprint.

Except as permitted under U.S. Copyright Law, no part of this book may be reprinted, reproduced, transmitted, or utilized in any form by any electronic, mechanical, or other means, now known or hereafter invented, including photocopying, microfilming, and recording, or in any information storage or retrieval system, without written permission from the publishers.

For permission to photocopy or use material electronically from this work, access www.copyright.com or contact the Copyright Clearance Center, Inc. (CCC), 222 Rosewood Drive, Danvers, MA 01923, 978-750-8400. For works that are not available on CCC please contact mpkbookspermissions@tandf.co.uk

Trademark notice: Product or corporate names may be trademarks or registered trademarks and are used only for identification and explanation without intent to infringe.

ISBN: 9781032550220 (hbk)
ISBN: 9781032550244 (pbk)
ISBN: 9781003428602 (ebk)

DOI: 10.1201/b23364

Typeset in Times
by KnowledgeWorks Global Ltd.

Contents

Acknowledgements

Natalie Heisler would like to acknowledge the co-supervision of her MA research in Political Science by Dr. Emmett Macfarlane and Dr. Maura R. Grossman at the University of Waterloo, Canada. Dr. Macfarlane's and Dr. Grossman's encouragement to pursue research in artificial intelligence at the intersection of rights and public policy, their guidance and their many helpful suggestions along the way, made this work possible. It was a privilege and a joy to work under the supervision of these scholars.

Natalie Heisler also expresses her thanks to all interview participants in this research, in particular to Benoit Deshaies, Gregg Blakely, and Wassim El-Kass whose insight and experience were invaluable to this work.

Maura R. Grossman's work is funded, in part, by the Natural Sciences and Engineering Research Council of Canada (NSERC).

The opinions expressed in this book are the authors' own and do not necessarily reflect the views of the institutions or organizations with which they are affiliated.

List of tables

List of abbreviations

3rd Review	Third review of the *Directive on Automated Decision-Making*
ADM	Automated decision-making
AI	Artificial intelligence
Charter	*Charter of Rights and Freedoms*
COE	Council of Europe
COMPAS	Correctional Offender Management Profiling for Alternative Sanctions
Digital Standards	Government of Canada Digital Standards
Directive	Government of Canada *Directive on Automated Decision-Making*
EU	European Union
EU AIA	European Union draft *Artificial Intelligence Act*
GDPR	European Union *General Data Protection Regulation*
IEEE	IEEE Standards Organization
IRCC	Immigration, Refugees and Citizenship Canada
ISO	International Organization for Standardization
ML	Machine learning
NIST	National Institute of Standards and Technology
PSOs	Public-sector organizations
RCMP	Royal Canadian Mounted Police
SCC	Supreme Court of Canada
SDOs	Standards development organizations
TBS	Treasury Board of Canada Secretariat
XAI	Explainable artificial intelligence

Introduction

1

This work seeks to make a contribution to human rights protections in the context of automated decision-making (ADM) by government. ADM is broadly defined as "technology that either assists or replaces the judgement of human decision-makers,"[1] and includes the use of machine learning (ML).[2] The Council of Europe (COE) offers the following definition of ML:

> A field of AI ["Artificial Intelligence"] made up of a set of techniques and algorithms that can be used to "train" a machine to automatically recognise patterns in a set of data. By recognising patterns in data, these machines can derive models that explain the data and/or predict future data. In summary, it is a machine that can learn without being explicitly programmed to perform the task.[3]

Governments use artificial intelligence (AI) and ML in ADM systems for a broad range of functions, including the administration and delivery of healthcare services, education, and housing benefits; for surveillance; and, within policing and criminal justice systems.[4] This trend is expected to grow

---

[1] Government of Canada Treasury Board Secretariat, 'Directive on Automated Decision-Making' (2021) <https://www.tbs-sct.gc.ca/pol/doc-eng.aspx?id=32592>. Appendix A: Definitions. The definition includes many examples of what is commonly known as AI within its definition of ADM, stating that: "These systems draw from fields like statistics, linguistics, and computer science, and use techniques such as rules-based systems, regression, predictive analytics, machine learning, deep learning, and neural nets."

[2] My use of ADM throughout this work is also meant to be inclusive of what is sometimes referred to in the literature as "algorithmic decision-making."

[3] Council of Europe Commissioner for Human Rights, 'Unboxing Artificial Intelligence: 10 Steps to Protect Human Rights' (2019) <https://www.coe.int/en/web/commissioner/-/unboxing-artificial-intelligence-10-steps-to-protect-human-rights> 24. The Council of Europe is Europe's largest human rights body based on state membership.

[4] For an overview of use cases, see e.g., Darrell M West and John R Allen, *Turning Point: Policymaking in the Era of Artificial Intelligence* (Brookings Institution Press 2020). See also: 'ADSs: Examples of Government Use Cases' (2019) <https://ainowinstitute.org/nycadschart.pdf>; AlgorithmWatch 'Automating Society Report 2020' (2020) <https://automatingsociety.algorithmwatch.org/wp-content/uploads/2020/10/

DOI: 10.1201/b23364-1

as governments seek innovative ways of improving both internal efficiencies and the speed and volume of client service delivery.[5] Raso cites the existing and "widespread" use of AI in the Canadian government's administrative context.[6]

ADM has been controversial for its human rights impacts. An extensive study by the COE concluded that AI has the potential to impact human rights and fundamental freedoms, including but not limited to the right to be free from discrimination; the right to due process; and, the right to privacy, freedom of expression, assembly and association.[7] In their survey of the use and impacts — including human rights impacts — of ADM across 16 European countries, the non-profit research organization AlgorithmWatch reported that "the vast majority of uses tend to put people at risk rather than help them."[8] Similarly, the UK government's Centre for Data Ethics and Innovation comprehensive report surveying both private and public sector uses of ADM, concluded that a rapidly growing number of examples were "inherently problematic" due to outcomes that were clearly unfair to those impacted by the decisions.[9] In Canada, the Law Commission of Ontario has uncovered many human rights concerns arising from the use of AI in their recent publications.[10]

Automating-Society-Report-2020.pdf>; Alexander Babuta and Marion Oswald, 'Data Analytics and Algorithmic Bias in Policing' (2019) <https://assets.publishing.service.gov. uk/government/uploads/system/uploads/attachment_data/file/831750/RUSI_Report_-_ Algorithms_and_Bias_in_Policing.pdf>; Virginia Eubanks, *Automating Inequality* (St Martin's Press 2017); Centre for Data Ethics and Innovation, 'Review into Bias in Algorithmic Decision-Making' (2020) <https://www.gov.uk/government/publications/ cdei-publishes-review-into-bias-in-algorithmic-decision-making>.

5 Maciej Kuziemski and Gianluca Misuraca, 'AI Governance in the Public Sector: Three Tales from the Frontiers of Automated Decision-Making in Democratic Settings' (2020) 44 Telecommunications Policy 101976 <https://linkinghub.elsevier.com/retrieve/pii/ S0308596120300689>.

6 Jennifer Raso, 'AI and Administrative Law' in Florian Martin-Bariteau and Teresa Scassa (eds), *Artificial Intelligence and the Law in Canada* (LexisNexis Canada Inc 2021) 181.

7 Council of Europe Committee of Experts on Internet Intermediaries (MSI-NET), 'Study on the Human Rights Dimensions of Automated Data Processing Techniques (In Particular Algorithms) and Possible Regulatory Implications.' (2018) <https://edoc.coe.int/en/ internet/7589-algorithms-and-human-rights-study-on-the-human-rights-dimensions-of- automated-data-processing-techniques-and-possible-regulatory-implications.html>.

8 AlgorithmWatch (n 4) 7.

9 Centre for Data Ethics and Innovation (n 4) 3.

10 See, e.g., Law Commission of Ontario, 'The Rise and Fall of AI and Algorithms in American Criminal Justice: Lessons for Canada' (2020) <https://www.lco-cdo.org/wp-content/ uploads/2020/10/Criminal-AI-Paper-Final-Oct-28-2020.pdf>. Additional Law Commission of Ontario publications are available at: https://www.lco-cdo.org/en/publications-papers/.

The mechanism of ML-based ADM that contributes to many of these concerns is disparate impact. The general definition of disparate impact — "practices that appear neutral on their face [that] may affect individuals and groups differently,"[11] — extends easily to ML-based ADM, i.e., ML is the "apparently neutral" practice whose resulting predictions may have the effect of disparate impact on those subject to ADM. Disparate impact may be desired, as in the case of taking deliberate actions to correct inequalities, and it may also reflect a true, explainable difference between groups such as in the context of sex-linked biological processes. But most of the concern with disparate impact in ADM systems is when ML functions in a way that is *not neutral*, producing unfair, unjustified outcomes.[12] We use the term "unjustified disparate impact" to describe the type of disparate impact that is the subject of this work, i.e., disparate impact "for which no operational justification is given."[13] Unless otherwise specified, disparate impact means unjustified disparate impact for the balance of this work.

The central question of this work is how should the use of ML-based ADM be regulated, in order to mitigate disparate impact and ensure that human rights — equality rights in particular — are not infringed upon? The regulatory landscape for ADM, in Canada and across the world, is far from settled. Legislative and policy models are emerging, and the role of standards is evolving to support regulatory objectives.

In this chapter, we begin by examining the preeminent legislative proposal, the European Union draft *Artificial Intelligence Act* (EU AIA)[14] and the role of standards in protecting human rights that it contemplates. We then contrast the structure and provisions of the EU AIA with Canada's

---

[11] Colleen Sheppard, *Inclusive Equality: The Relational Dimensions of Systemic Discrimination in Canada* (MQUP 2010) 19.

[12] David Danks and Alex John London, 'Algorithmic Bias in Autonomous Systems,' *Proceedings of the Twenty-Sixth International Joint Conference on Artificial Intelligence (IJCAI-17)* (2017) <https://www.researchgate.net/profile/Alex-London/publication/318830422_Algorithmic_Bias_in_Autonomous_Systems/links/5a4bb017aca2729b7c893d1b/Algorithmic-Bias-in-Autonomous-Systems.pdf>. See also: Centre for Data Ethics and Innovation (n 4).

[13] This is an adaptation of the IEEE definition of unjustified bias to unjustified disparate impact. See Ansgar Koene, Liz Dowthwaite and Suchana Seth, 'IEEE P7003™ Standard for Algorithmic Bias Considerations,' *Proceedings of the International Workshop on Software Fairness* (ACM 2018) <https://dl.acm.org/doi/10.1145/3194770.3194773> 39.

[14] European Commission, 'Proposal for a REGULATION OF THE EUROPEAN PARLIAMENT AND OF THE COUNCIL LAYING DOWN HARMONISED RULES ON ARTIFICIAL INTELLIGENCE (ARTIFICIAL INTELLIGENCE ACT) AND AMENDING CERTAIN UNION LEGISLATIVE ACTS' (2021) <https://digital-strategy.ec.europa.eu/en/library/proposal-regulation-european-approach-artificial-intelligence>.

federal regulatory instrument, the *Directive on Automated Decision-Making*[15] (Directive), locating standards as an element of soft law in the administrative decision-making context to which the Directive applies. We define and explain the links between machine learning, algorithmic bias, and disparate impact and the guarantee of substantive equality in the *Charter of Rights and Freedoms*[16] (*Charter*) demonstrating that standards to control algorithmic bias are needed for equality rights protection. This introductory material is then synthesized to present the central argument of this work, that standards must be derived from legal principles and precedent. The research question to be addressed in this work is:

> In the context of the Directive, what standards can be derived from legal principles and precedent for the control of algorithmic bias in machine learning in order to mitigate disparate impact in administrative decisions?

This chapter concludes by providing methodological details, assumptions, and scoping decisions.

1.1 REGULATION OF ARTIFICIAL INTELLIGENCE: THE EUROPEAN CONTEXT

The EU AIA — introduced into the European Union (EU) parliament in April 2021 — requires agreement on its text by the EU parliament and the COE before it can pass into law.[17] At the time of writing, this work remains in progress. Widely understood as the most comprehensive legislation for AI anywhere in the world to date,[18] and applicable to both private and public sectors,[19] it states several objectives for the regulation of

---

[15] Government of Canada Treasury Board Secretariat, 'Directive on Automated Decision-Making' (n 1).

[16] Constitution Act, 1982.

[17] Future of Life Institute, 'The AI Act: Developments' (2022) <https://artificialintelligenceact. eu/developments/>.

[18] Law Commission of Ontario, 'Comparing European and Canadian AI Regulation' (2021) <https://www.lco-cdo.org/wp-content/uploads/2021/12/Comparing-European-and-Canadian-AI-Regulation-Final-November-2021.pdf> 31.

[19] Ibid. 16.

AI systems. These objectives collectively address concern for safety of AI systems, calling for the respect and enforcement of fundamental rights,[20] and the creation of a single regulated EU market for AI systems.[21] The EU AIA defines specific aspects of AI risk it seeks to regulate, enumerates AI systems it deems to conflict with EU values, enables oversight bodies, and delineates how entities would achieve compliance with its requirements. It mandates the development of new standards[22] for AI systems that are integrated with existing regional or national sector-specific regulation (e.g., environment, health, finance) where applicable, and includes specific requirements for circumstances falling outside of existing regulation. It is a lengthy, complex legislative proposal that generated great volumes of critical reaction soon after it was proposed, diminutively summed up as "predictably ... mixed."[23]

We will not attempt to cover the full scope of this reaction, rather we will highlight two key observations relevant to the protection of fundamental rights. First, with respect to the role of technical standards in upholding fundamental rights, the EU AIA states that standards must be " ... consistent with the Charter of fundamental rights of the European Union (the Charter) and should be non-discriminatory and in line with the Union's international trade commitments."[24] Yet, critics observe that standards are often developed without the participation of stakeholders knowledgeable in fundamental rights, elaborating that "standardization procedures tend to be opaque, prone

---

[20] "Fundamental rights" are defined as those included in the European Union Charter of Fundamental Rights, which expands upon, and includes by reference, the European Convention on Human Rights (ECHR). See: European Commission (n 14) 11.

[21] Ibid. 3.

[22] In general, standards are criteria put in place to meet a stated regulatory objective. Standards can take many different forms. They can refer to substantial or procedural elements, and can be voluntary or mandatory. A standard also refers to an asset created by a standards developing organization, i.e., documentation that articulates a set of principle-based and/or operational requirements to adhere to a stated objective. The EU AIA contemplates various types of technical standards (including technical specifications) in various circumstances; for a complete discussion of the role of technical standards and specifications in the EU AIA regulation see: Mark McFadden and others, 'Harmonising Artificial Intelligence: The Role of Standards in the EU AI Regulation' (2021) <https://oxcaigg.oii.ox.ac.uk/wp-content/uploads/sites/124/2021/12/Harmonising-AI-OXIL.pdf>. For the purpose of this work, the general description of standards provided in this footnote will suffice and will be used to describe AI standards.

[23] Marietje Schaake, 'The European Commission's Artificial Intelligence Act' (2021) <https://hai.stanford.edu/sites/default/files/2021-06/HAI_Issue-Brief_The-European-Commissions-Artificial-Intelligence-Act.pdf> 2.

[24] European Commission (n 14) 20.

to industry lobbying, and hardly accessible to all relevant stakeholders—especially not to civil society and those affected."[25] Further, the standards development organizations (SDOs) to which the EU AIA would delegate the development of technical standards for AI — namely CEN, the European Committee for Standardization; and CENELEC, the European Committee for Electrotechnical Standardization — are private organizations whose rule-making authority in the realm of human rights (rules to which both private and public actors would be held accountable) is unclear.[26] In other words, while standards are clearly positioned as a channel to human rights protections in the EU AIA, they are largely non-existent today and there is some doubt that the accepted means by which they are developed will lead to the desired outcome.

Second, despite its objectives spanning the respect for fundamental rights, the EU AIA has been criticized because it neither grants rights to individuals impacted by AI[27] nor does it contain any binding obligations for the protection of rights.[28] For this reason, some commentators have cast a dim view on the legislation's effectiveness for human rights protections.[29] We introduced the EU AIA to illustrate the model it proposes for the protection of human rights and the role of standards it envisions. And being the first legislation of its kind — a pan-European regulatory model purporting to drive both market and human rights objectives — it has been much studied in the literature. Yet even the early critiques point to the weakness of its provisions and controversy in its reliance upon standards that do not yet exist for the protection of human rights. It prompts one to consider how AI regulation in Canada, structured on a much different model of policy versus legislation, comparatively serves to protect human rights.

---

[25] AlgorithmWatch, 'Draft AI Act: EU Needs to Live up to Its Own Ambitions in Terms of Governance and Enforcement' (2021) <https://algorithmwatch.org/en/eu-ai-act-consultation-submission-2021/#:~:text=Newsletters-,Draft AI Act%3A EU needs to live up to its,transparency requirements and enforcement mechanisms.> 5–6.

[26] Michael Veale and Frederik Zuiderveen Borgesius, 'Demystifying the Draft EU Artificial Intelligence Act — Analysing the Good, the Bad, and the Unclear Elements of the Proposed Approach' (2021) 22 Computer law review international 97, 105–106.

[27] European Digital Rights (EDRi) and others, 'An EU Artificial Intelligence Act for Fundamental Rights: A Civil Society Statement' (2021) <https://algorithmwatch.org/en/eu-artificial-intelligence-act-for-fundamental-rights/#:~:text=The EU's Artificial Intelligence Act,is set out to achieve> 4.

[28] Law Commission of Ontario (n 18) 32.

[29] Ibid.

1.2 REGULATION OF ARTIFICIAL INTELLIGENCE: THE CANADIAN ADMINISTRATIVE CONTEXT

With the exception of *Bill 64* which passed in the National Assembly of Québec in September 2021 and is not yet in effect at the time of writing,[30] Canada has not yet enacted legislation for the regulation of AI.[31] However, it was among the first countries to establish a mandatory policy applicable to AI. On April 1, 2019, the *Directive on Automated Decision-Making* took effect. ADM is defined in the Directive as a "technology that either assists or replaces the judgement of human decision-makers," and includes AI within the scope of the technology that comprise an ADM system.[32] The Directive is applicable only to federal administrative bodies to whom authority and decision-making power has been granted through legislation. And it is applicable only to their use of ADM for administrative decisions, defined as decisions that affect the "legal rights, privileges or interests"[33] of an external client (i.e., individuals or groups external to government).[34]

---

[30] Bill 64: An Act to modernize legislative provisions as regards the protection of personal information. 2021 (see: https://m.assnat.qc.ca/en/travaux-parlementaires/projets-loi/projet-loi-64-42-1.html). The specific provisions of this bill that relate to AI are those applicable to the use of personal information to make a decision impacting an individual solely via automated processing, by both private and public entities in sections 12.1 and 65.2 respectively. In this circumstance, individuals are entitled to be informed, upon request, of: (1) of the personal information used to render the decision; (2) of the reasons and the principal factors and parameters that led to the decision; and (3) of the right of the person concerned to have the personal information used to render the decision corrected.

[31] Michael Geist, 'AI and International Regulation' in Florian Martin-Bariteau and Teresa Scassa (eds), *Artificial Intelligence and the Law in Canada* (LexisNexis Canada Inc 2021). 370–373. In June, 2022, Bill C-27 was introduced at the federal level (see: https://www.parl.ca/legisinfo/en/bill/44-1/c-27?view=details#bill-profile-tabs). Bill C-27 both amends existing privacy legislation and includes new regulatory requirements pertaining to artificial intelligence systems. At the time of writing, Bill C-27 was in second reading in the House of Commons.

[32] Government of Canada Treasury Board Secretariat, 'Directive on Automated Decision-Making' (n 1). Appendix A: Definitions. The definition includes many examples of what is commonly known as AI within its definition of ADM, stating that: "These systems draw from fields like statistics, linguistics, and computer science, and use techniques such as rules-based systems, regression, predictive analytics, machine learning, deep learning, and neural nets."

[33] Ibid.

[34] 'Interview with Benoit Deshaies, Director, Data and Artificial Intelligence, Office of the Chief Information Officer, Treasury Board of Canada Secretariat, Government of Canada (Toronto, Canada, 27 November 2020).'

The responsibilities of administrative bodies — that are variously referred to as agencies, commissions, boards, or tribunals[35] — span a wide variety of specialized public functions, at all levels of government. Administrative bodies may perform one or more of the following functions: advising government; carrying out operational functions for government; developing rules and policies; creating and enforcing legally binding regulations; proposing legislation; and adjudicating disputes.[36] Under federal jurisdiction, for example, administrative boards include the National Parole Board, the Social Security Tribunal of Canada, and the Canadian Industrial Relations Board, and there are more than 25 commissions, tribunals, and adjudication panels across Canada relating to human rights.[37] Administrative bodies develop and apply rules within the limits of their legislatively defined authority to uphold a statutory or policy objective. Those rules are then applied in a forward-looking manner to make day-to-day decisions within the authority of the administrative body. Administrative bodies apply a myriad of rules and adjudicative processes that affect a great number of individuals in both volume and in consequence.[38]

In addition to the development and application of rules, administrative bodies are responsible for discretionary decision-making. Discretionary decisions are those in which the decision-maker is not obliged to fulfil any particular outcome, and instead use their expertise to weigh the facts and circumstances of a particular case to arrive at a decision within the scope of the applicable law.[39] Most statutes grant administrative bodies wide powers of discretionary decision-making,[40] and in practice, the distinction between the application of rules and discretionary decision-making blurs as explained in *Baker v. Canada*: "Most administrative decisions involve the exercise of implicit discretion in relation to many aspects of decision-making."[41] For individuals subject to administrative decision-making, this

---

[35] Thomas S Kuttner, 'Administrative Tribunals in Canada' (*The Canadian Encyclopedia*, 2020) <https://www.thecanadianencyclopedia.ca/en/article/administrative-tribunals#:-:text= Tribunals are set up by,between people and the government.>.

[36] Lorne Sossin and Emily Lawrence, *Administrative Law in Practice: Principles and Advocacy* (Emond Publishing 2018) 40–41.

[37] Pearl Eliadis, *Speaking Out on Human Rights: Debating Canada's Human Rights System* (MQUP 2014). Appendix Three.

[38] Colleen M Flood and Jennifer Dolling, 'A Historical Map for Administrative Law: There Be Dragons' in Colleen M Flood and Lorne Sossin (eds), *Administrative Law in Context* (Third, Emond Montgomery Publications Limited 2018) 3.

[39] *Baker v. Minister of Citizenship and Immigration* [1999] 2 SCR 817. 820 (hereinafter "*Baker*")

[40] Sossin and Lawrence (n 36) 27.

[41] *Baker v. Minister of Citizenship and Immigration* (n 39) 854.

means that their unique circumstances can be considered in this discretionary context, that it need not be a "one size fits all" approach — in this way, discretionary decision-making is an important tool for ensuring equitable outcomes.[42]

Administrative bodies typically possess expertise in legislative interpretation relevant to the functions they perform,[43] as well as domain-specific, technical expertise.[44] This specialized expertise is used to develop supporting "soft-law" instruments that are not legally binding but are used to inform both the procedure and substance of the administrative body's discretionary decisions. Soft law includes such elements as training manuals, standards, and guidelines,[45] and even more informal elements such as "oral directive[s] or simply ... ingrained administrative culture."[46] The standards we will propose in this work would be considered soft law.

Much of the work of administrative bodies intersects with *Charter* rights, and administrative bodies play a critical role in either upholding or eroding individual rights, as noted by scholar Colleen Sheppard: "in some cases, judges have focused on administrative law as the most appropriate source of protection for ensuring government accountability and respect for human rights."[47] What precisely does this mean in the context of the Directive and ADM — which human rights are meant to be respected, how is administrative law a channel for this, and what is the role of standards? We address these questions in this work, focusing on equality rights. Before proceeding, we will provide additional, necessary context: In Sections 1.3 and 1.4, we will describe the link between ADM and equality rights; and in Section 1.5, we will elaborate on standards.

---

[42] Kenneth Culp Davis, *Discretionary Justice; a Preliminary Inquiry.* (Louisiana State University Press 1969), as cited in Gus Van Harten and others, *Administrative Law: Cases, Text, and Materials* (Seventh, Emond Montgomery Publications Limited 2015) 920–922.

[43] *Edmonton (City) v. Edmonton East (Capilano) Shopping Centres Ltd* [2016] 2 SCR 293, 295 as cited in Mary Liston, 'Administering the Canadian Rule of Law' in Colleen M Flood and Lorne Sossin (eds), *Administrative Law in Context* (Third, Emond Montgomery Publications Limited 2018) 169.

[44] Andrew Green, 'Delegation and Consultation: How the Administrative State Functions and the Importance of Rules' in Colleen M Flood and Lorne Sossin (eds), *Administrative Law in Context* (Emond Montgomery Publications Limited 2018) 327.

[45] Ibid. 313.

[46] Lorne Sossin, 'Discretion Unbound: Reconciling the Charter and Soft Law' (2002), 45 Canadian public administration 465, 467.

[47] Sheppard (n 11) 64.

1.3 EQUALITY RIGHTS: DISPARATE IMPACT IN ADM

In a typical ML-based ADM system, according to the COE's definition of ML provided in the introductory pages of this work, ML generates predictions that are then used as information in the decision-making process. The words prediction and inference are sometimes used interchangeably, but we will differentiate between the two, using the word *prediction* to refer to a statistical computation and using the word *inference* to describe the way in which the prediction is interpreted, either by a human or as part of an ADM system. When disparate impact in the ML-based predictions results in inferences or outcomes that affect protected individuals or groups differently — for example, groups defined on the basis of race, religion, or sex — it can amount to a human rights violation as will be described in the case example that follows.

1.3.1 Case Study: Disparate Impact in the COMPAS ADM

One high-profile example of disparate impact in ADM systems was exposed in 2016, when the Correctional Offender Management Profiling for Alternative Sanctions (COMPAS) algorithmic risk assessment system was the subject of a challenge in the Wisconsin Supreme Court (*State v. Loomis*).[48] The COMPAS system was developed in 1998 for use in pretrial risk and needs assessments;[49] however, in 2012, judges began to use the COMPAS predictions of recidivism as inputs to their sentencing decisions in the State of Wisconsin.[50] The COMPAS ADM system is used to inform judges about an offender's risk of recidivism, based on a combination of publicly available data and personal data about the offender, which compare the individual to group trends and thus produce a risk score.[51]

---

[48]   *State v. Loomis* 881 N.W.2d 749 (Wis 2016).

[49]   Christine S Scott-Hayward, *Punishing Poverty: How Bail and Pretrial Detention Fuel Inequalities in the Criminal Justice System* (University of California Press 2019) 91–92.

[50]   Park A, 'Injustice Ex Machina: Predictive Algorithms in Criminal Sentencing' (2019) *UCLA Law Review Law Meets World* <https://www.uclalawreview.org/injustice-ex-machina-pre-dictive-algorithms-in-criminal-sentencing/> para 4.

[51]   In *State v. Loomis*, it was argued that the use of COMPAS interfered with the defendant's

The case garnered much public attention and a subsequent independent analysis of the data and algorithm used by the COMPAS system uncovered its disparate impact. In their study, investigative journalists from ProPublica found that the COMPAS system propagated racial disparities, incorrectly predicting that Black offenders were twice as likely to reoffend, compared with White offenders.[52] ProPublica showed the prediction to be incorrect by examining data not considered by the COMPAS system, specifically historical records of actual rates of recidivism,[53] and concluded that the COMPAS system's algorithm had systematically predicted Black offenders' rates of recidivism to be higher than actual, documented rates of recidivism. Further, ProPublica found that inaccurate predictions have real impacts on offenders when judges draw inferences from the predicted rate of recidivism — for example, when judges infer that higher predicted rates of recidivism for Black offenders should mean longer prison sentences.[54] The algorithm's incorrect prediction for Black offenders (i.e., of a higher likelihood to reoffend) was found to be a contributing factor to the unjustified disparate impact (i.e., longer prison sentences than similar White offenders).

The discovery by ProPublica of the mechanism of disparate impact at play for Black offenders aptly illustrates how disparate impact interferes with human rights — specifically equality rights — because the COMPAS algorithm created outcomes unfairly differentiated by race.

---

constitutional due process rights by denying him an individualized sentence, see: 'Criminal Law - Sentencing Guidelines - Wisconsin Supreme Court Requires Warning before Use of Algorithmic Risk Assessments in Sentencing - State v. Loomis.(Case Note)' (2017) 130 Harvard Law Review. 1530 <https://harvardlawreview.org/2017/03/state-v-loomis/#:~:text=the%20Wisconsin%20Supreme%20Court%20held,court%20nor%20to%20the%20defendant>. In a decision that has been highly criticized in the academic literature, the defendant lost his claim of a due process violation when the Court concluded that he could challenge his recidivism risk score because he would be aware of his own data contributions to the risk calculations. In fact, it would be impossible for Mr. Loomis to reconstruct the reasoning behind his recidivism score due to the complexity and opacity of the COMPAS algorithms, see: Sascha van Schendel, 'The Challenges of Risk Profiling Used by Law Enforcement: Examining the Cases of COMPAS and SyRI' in Leonie Reins (ed), *Regulating New Technologies in Uncertain Times* (Springer-Verlag Berlin Heidelberg 2019). Despite the defendant losing the due process claim, the case has been widely cited for the implication of the COMPAS system in disparate impact.

[52] Julia Angwin and others, 'Machine Bias' (*ProPublica*, 2016) <https://www.propublica.org/article/machine-bias-risk-assessments-in-criminal-sentencing>.

[53] Jeff Larson and others, 'How We Analyzed the COMPAS Recidivism Algorithm' (*ProPublica*, 2016) <https://www.propublica.org/article/how-we-analyzed-the-compas-recidivism-algorithm>.

[54] Angwin and others (n 52).

1.4 SITUATING DISPARATE IMPACT IN THE *CHARTER*

How is disparate impact situated within *Charter* equality rights guarantees of non-discrimination? Section 15 of the *Charter* states that:

1. Every individual is equal before and under the law and has the right to the equal protection and equal benefit of the law without discrimination and, in particular, without discrimination based on race, national or ethnic origin, colour, religion, sex, age or mental or physical disability.
2. Subsection (1) does not preclude any law, program, or activity that has as its object the amelioration of conditions of disadvantaged individuals or groups including those that are disadvantaged because of race, national or ethnic origin, colour, religion, sex, age or mental or physical disability.

In *Andrews*, the first *Charter* equality rights case to make it to the Supreme Court of Canada (SCC) in 1989, section 15(1) was interpreted to guarantee not only formal equality based on equal treatment, but also equality based on the *effects* of laws even if the treatment is equal.[55] The SCC's interpretation of section 15 as upholding substantive equality — where the focus shifts from equal treatment to "equitable outcomes"[56] — has remained consistent in the years that have elapsed.[57] As elaborated in *Kapp*: "Section 15(1) and s. 15(2) work together to promote the vision of substantive equality that underlies s. 15 as a whole."[58] These guarantees apply not only to laws, they apply to a wide variety of government policies and actions, including administrative decisions, meaning that administrative decisions must not interfere in any unlawful manner with equality rights.[59] It follows that decision-makers using ADM must be vigilant to ensure that the outcomes of their decisions will not produce disparate impact leading to discriminatory outcomes.

---

[55] *Andrews v. Law Society of British Columbia* [1989] 1 SCR 143, 145.
[56] Sheppard (n 11) 8.
[57] Government of Canada Department of Justice, 'Section 15 – Equality Rights' (*Charterpedia*, 2022) <https://www.justice.gc.ca/eng/csj-sjc/rfc-dlc/ccrf-ccdl/check/art15.html>.
[58] *R. v. Kapp* [2008] 2 SCR 483 para 16.
[59] Government of Canada Department of Justice (n 57).

1.5 THE ROLE OF STANDARDS IN PROTECTING HUMAN RIGHTS

There is no one perfect model to regulate AI for the protection of human rights. The EU AIA legislation in the broad context of AI systems spanning public and private sectors makes a strong call for the protection of human rights but specific standards and provisions for doing so remain to be seen. Like the EU AIA, the Canadian Directive does not create any directly enforceable rights.[60] Instead it states in the preamble that: "The Government is committed to [utilizing artificial intelligence] in a manner that is compatible with core administrative law principles such as transparency, accountability, legality, and procedural fairness."[61] The EU AIA has not yet been enacted, so how it stands up to judicial review for human rights protection remains to be seen. Similarly, in Canada, as of late 2021, scholars confirmed the "absence of case law addressing algorithmic decision-making,"[62] and other commentators report the same around the globe, that cases that consider the legality of ML-based ADM systems are few.[63] At the time of writing, neither model has yet been tested for its human rights teeth.

The lack of precedent established through judicial review, and the slow pace at which it is likely to be established in future, increases the practical urgency that controls to mitigate disparate impact in ADM must be established now, that proverbially get it right the first time, and that provide protection against known harms. How can such controls be achieved? In short, mitigating disparate impact in ML-based ADM amounts to controlling the processes that produce it in the first place — controlling what is known as algorithmic bias in ML.

Bias is a general term that describes a difference between the characterization of an entity (e.g., person, idea, institution, thing) and its true nature. Bias is not necessarily a deliberate misrepresentation, it may arise due to unknown or misunderstood factors. In social science, bias is closely connected to the concept of measurement validity, i.e., "the extent to which an empirical measure adequately reflects the real meaning of the concept

---

[60] Teresa Scassa, 'Administrative Law and the Governance of Automated Decision-Making: A Critical Look at Canada's Directive on Automated Decision-Making' (2021) 54 UBC Law Review 251, 268

[61] Government of Canada Treasury Board Secretariat, 'Directive on Automated Decision-Making' (n 1). Preamble.

[62] Raso (n 6) 181.

[63] Law Commission of Ontario (n 10). See also, Centre for Data Ethics and Innovation (n 4).

under consideration."[64] The term *algorithmic bias* encompasses the ways in which the model and its predictions can differ from the true patterns they are intended to capture. Recall the general definition of disparate impact provided earlier — "practices that appear neutral on their face [that] may affect individuals and groups differently,"[65] — where ML was described as the "*apparently* neutral" practice whose resulting predictions have the effect of disparate impact on those subject to ADM. Where algorithmic bias is present, ML is the *non-neutral* process that transforms input data into predictions.[66]

Algorithmic bias can arise due to numerous factors, categorized as systemic factors, human factors, and statistical and computational factors.[67] Systemic factors encompass historical, societal, or institutional practices[68] occurring anywhere in the ML lifecycle from pre-design to design and development, to deployment.[69] Human factors include individual and group behaviours and well-known cognitive biases (e.g., confirmation bias, groupthink, Rashomon effect) that influence the ML lifecycle and thus contribute to algorithmic bias.[70] Statistical and computational factors refer to characteristics of the data and algorithms in the pre-design and design and development stages of the ML lifecycle.[71] Algorithmic bias can result in an advantage for some — such as when a biased prediction results in a better outcome than would have otherwise occurred — and a disadvantage for others. Controls must be established for the factors that contribute to algorithmic bias, in order to avoid the outcome of disparate impact and ensure that its use for administrative decision-making is fair to all those impacted.

Mandating compliance with standards across the ML lifecycle is one mechanism for the control of algorithmic bias. Recall the EU AIA mandate

---

[64] Earl R Babbie, *The Practice of Social Research* (13th ed., Wadsworth Cengage Learning 2013) 191

[65] Sheppard (n 11) 19.

[66] Danks and London (n 12) 1491. See also Reva Schwartz and others, 'Towards a Standard for Identifying and Managing Bias in Artificial Intelligence' (2022) <https://nvlpubs.nist.gov/nistpubs/SpecialPublications/NIST.SP.1270.pdf>.

[67] Schwartz and others (n 66) 6–9.

[68] Ibid.

[69] The National Institute of Standards and Technology (NIST) has proposed a three-stage lifecycle approach within which to examine algorithmic bias: "PRE-DESIGN: where the technology is devised, defined, and elaborated; DESIGN AND DEVELOPMENT: where the technology is constructed; and DEPLOYMENT: where technology is used by, or applied to, various individuals or groups." (see Reva Schwartz and others, 'A Proposal for Identifying and Managing Bias in Artificial Intelligence' (2021) <https://nvlpubs.nist.gov/nistpubs/SpecialPublications/NIST.SP.1270-draft.pdf>. 6) Unless otherwise specified, when lifecycle is referred to in this work, it is assumed to be describing the NIST lifecycle.

[70] Schwartz and others (n 66) 8.

[71] Ibid. 9.

for the development of standards for AI systems. Likewise, it would be prudent for administrative bodies in Canada to adopt standards to control algorithmic bias in their use of ADM to mitigate disparate impact. The Directive's formal policy language does not contain any specific standards, nor is it the intention for it to do so.[72] Rather, in keeping with administrative law, the Directive contains procedural requirements that must be fulfilled by agencies using ADM in order to comply with the Directive:

> 6.3.1 Before launching into production, developing processes so that the data and information used by the Automated Decision Systems are tested for unintended data biases and other factors that may unfairly impact the outcomes.
>
> 6.3.2 Developing processes to monitor the outcomes of Automated Decision Systems to safeguard against unintentional outcomes and to verify compliance with institutional and program legislation, as well as this Directive, on a scheduled basis.[73]

And in the federal Policy on Service and Digital, under whose authority the Directive was issued, the additional applicable requirements include:

> 4.4.2.4.1 Ensuring decisions produced using these systems are efficient, accountable, and unbiased; and,
>
> 4.4.2.4.2 Ensuring transparency and disclosure regarding use of the systems and ongoing assessment and management of risks.[74]

The language in the above-mentioned requirements is deceptively simple. Understanding what bias is and how it is manifested in data and algorithms is an active area of academic and industry research — much of which is befittingly interdisciplinary spanning computer science, sociotechnical,[75] and legal domains — but at the same time struggles for a lack of a unifying taxonomy. Approaches for the control of bias are highly varied, shaped by

---

[72] 'Interview with Benoit Deshaies, Director, Data and Artificial Intelligence, Office of the Chief Information Officer, Treasury Board of Canada Secretariat, Government of Canada (Toronto, Canada, 27 November 2020).' (n 34).

[73] Government of Canada Treasury Board Secretariat, 'Directive on Automated Decision-Making' (n 1).

[74] Government of Canada Treasury Board Secretariat, 'Policy on Service and Digital' <https://www.tbs-sct.gc.ca/pol/doc-eng.aspx?id=32603>.

[75] Socio-technical research domains focus on systems that include "a combination of technical and human or natural elements" (see: SEBok: Guide to the Systems Engineering Body of Knowledge, 'Sociotechnical System (Glossary)' (2022) <https://www.sebokwiki.org/wiki/Sociotechnical_System_(glossary)>.)

the specific context within which ML is being applied — it is far from being a settled methodology. Further, take the mention of "unbiased" in the Policy on Service and Digital Section 4.4.2.4.1 — bias is a matter of degree, not a yes/no matter, which then implies the question of how much bias is tolerable within a particular context of government policy objectives. There are many more questions than cookbook answers to the control of bias today. Yet, it's clear that the Treasury Board of Canada Secretariat (TBS) — the author of these instruments — is mandating the control for bias[76] in processes and outcomes.

Against this backdrop, how can standards help in protecting against human rights violations that arise from algorithmic bias? Benoit Deshaies, Director, Data and Artificial Intelligence at TBS who, at the time of writing, leads the ongoing work of the Directive explained that there is a place for standards to complement the Directive: federal agencies are free to establish their own policies and standards in their use of ADM that are most relevant to their objectives and use cases.[77] Standards could also be included in TBS-authored supplementary guidelines on the interpretation and implementation of the Directive's requirements.

Developing standards for algorithmic bias is an active area of research today. Consider, for example,, the work of the International Organization for Standardization (ISO),[78] the IEEE Standards Organization (IEEE)[79] — both widely known for the development of international standards — and the National Institute of Standards and Technology (NIST) whose scope is the United States. At the time of writing, NIST is working towards a consensus-based technical standard described in their publication titled *Towards a Standard for Identifying and Managing Bias in Artificial Intelligence.*[80] In late 2021, the ISO published the standard *Bias in AI Systems and AI aided decision making,*[81] and the in-progress *IEEE P7003™ Standard for*

---

[76]   The use of the term 'bias' in 6.3.1 of the Directive is used to refer to data bias specifically, which contributes to the outcome of algorithmic bias. The use of 'unbiased' in 4.4.2.4.1 of the Policy is unqualified. We assume that all the above quoted references to bias fall within what we are referring to throughout this work as algorithmic bias.

[77]   'Interview with Benoit Deshaies, Director, Data and Artificial Intelligence, Office of the Chief Information Officer, Treasury Board of Canada Secretariat, Government of Canada (Toronto, Canada, 27 November 2020).' (n 34).

[78]   International Organization for Standardization, 'ISO in Brief' (2019) <https://www.iso.org/files/live/sites/isoorg/files/store/en/PUB100007.pdf> 3.

[79]   IEEE, 'IEEE Standards' (2021) <https://www.ieee.org/standards/index.html>.

[80]   Schwartz and others (n 66).

[81]   International Organization for Standardization, 'ISO/IEC DTR 24027 Information Technology — Artificial Intelligence (AI) – Bias in AI Systems and AI Aided Decision Making' (2021) <https://www.iso.org/standard/77607.html?browse=tc>.

Algorithmic Bias Considerations aims to provide practical guidelines, procedures, and criteria that can be used in designing and building AI applications is in progress.[82] While these standards are voluntary, if they are adopted in legislation, they become legally binding. Even when not legally binding, once an organization chooses to adopt a voluntary standard, the organization's compliance or lack thereof with that standard is relevant should legal disputes arise.

Should the NIST, IEEE, ISO, or other standards be adopted on a voluntary basis by federal government agencies using ADM? The answer is not immediately obvious. Recall the concerns raised by commentators in response to the EU AIA, that the development of standards often lacks the necessary input and authority of those with expertise in human rights. Scholars have also pointed out that the work of some of the SDOs, such as the IEEE, is performed by volunteers without any required accreditation for their participation, and who bring their own biases and interests to the standards development exercise.[83] Standards created by SDOs are often done so by and for practitioners who are sensitive to the technical characteristics of AI systems. In short, standards arising out of the SDOs — which can make important contributions to solving real practical problems — are not necessarily designed to be grounded in, nor do they emerge from, human rights or other legal norms.

A recent article by scholar Gillian Hadfield expertly summarized the differences in AI governance schemes based on the source from which they are derived.[84] Hadfield contrasted the development of explainable AI (XAI) techniques which help developers understand in technical terms how algorithms work, with the need for justifiable AI which helps those impacted by algorithmic decisions understand both the factors used to make a decision that impacts them and whether those factors have some basis in legal and societal norms. Standards developed by SDOs thus far emphasize the former with little attention to the latter.

Does this mean that the work of SDOs should be dismissed by TBS or by Canadian federal agencies in their efforts to implement ADM? Not at all. The aforementioned published standards and the technical communities facilitated by the SDOs offer resources and material that administrative bodies can and should consult when considering standards for algorithmic bias. However, we

---

[82] Interview with Gerlinde Weger, Director, Member of the IEEE P7003™ Working Group (Toronto, Canada, 26 April 2021). See also: Koene, Dowthwaite and Seth (n 13).

[83] Paula Boddington, 'Normative Modes: Codes and Standards', *Oxford Handbook of Ethics of AI* (Oxford University Press 2020) 130.

[84] Gillian K Hadfield, 'Explanation and Justification: AI Decision-Making, Law, and the Rights of Citizens' (2021) <https://srinstitute.utoronto.ca/news/hadfield-justifiable-ai>.

agree with Hadfield's assessment that: "We want to know that the decisions that affect us are justifiable according to the rules and norms of our society."[85] In this work, we narrow this sentiment further and argue that the rationale for adopting standards must be clearly and logically drawn, stemming from the law. And the premise for this work is that if such standards can be implemented, this would help to reduce future complaints *by*, and would proactively enable human rights protections *for*, subjects of ML-based ADM.[86]

There are several other justifications for this approach in addition to Hadfield's reasoning. First, because federal agencies — equally in their use of ADM as in any other capacity — must adhere to administrative law principles and uphold *Charter* guarantees including that of substantive equality. Notwithstanding the unknown circumstances of a future complaint, adopting standards based on legal principles could help to ensure that the administrative decisions made using those standards would be deemed sound should they be subject to judicial review. In their work developing policy guidelines for the use of ADM, this is what Immigration, Refugees and Citizenship Canada (IRCC) described as the need for "defensible decision-making."[87] Scholar Paul Daly generalizes this concept in his discussion of "artificial administration" — government use of technology and AI to assist or replace human decision-makers — in which the author cautions that "if artificial administration is implemented without regard for the norms of administrative law the decisions it produces will simply be unlawful."[88]

Daly further proposes that embedding the norms of administrative law into the processes of artificial administration would increase the "social acceptability" of these government practices.[89] At the time of writing, only ten completed Algorithmic Impact Assessments — a key requirement of the Directive — have been recorded.[90] And while we do not dispute Daly's

---

[85] Ibid. para 15.

[86] Similarly, Kroll states that: "incorporating nondiscrimination in the initial design of algorithms is the safest path that decisionmakers can take, and we should encourage the development and deployment of technical tools to aid in that design." See: Joshua A Kroll and others, 'Accountable Algorithms' (2017) 165 The University of Pennsylvania Law Review 633, 695.

[87] Immigration Refugees and Citizenship Canada, 'Policy Playbook for Automated Support for Decision-Making' (2021) <https://gccollab.ca/groups/profile/7211943/enircc-digital-policy-guidancefrorientation-stratu00e9gique-du2019ircc-sur-le-numu00e9rique> 33.

[88] Paul Daly, 'Artificial Administration: Administrative Law in the Age of Machines' [2019] SSRN Electronic Journal <https://www.ssrn.com/abstract=3493381> 7.

[89] Ibid.

[90] Government of Canada, 'Algorithmic Impact Assessment (AIA)' (2023) <https://www.canada.ca/en/government/system/digital-government/digital-government-innovations/responsible-use-ai/algorithmic-impact-assessment.html#toc3-3>. See Section 3.3 which states that "Departments are responsible for releasing the final results of the [Algorithmic

assertion, the more immediate problem could be lack of engagement with the Directive, which could mean that few federal agencies are pursuing the use of ADM. Given the potential for efficiencies and improved outcomes that ADM is said to enable for government,[91] this seems like a lost opportunity. Putting in place standards to assist agencies in complying with the Directive could help make it easier to adopt ADM, knowing that agencies' efforts to do so would be legal and fair.

The implied assumption is that administrative law is in fact a sufficient source for this task, meaning that legal principles and precedent provide the tools needed to grapple with the problem of control of algorithmic bias and the outcome of disparate impact in ADM systems. Scholars are beginning to acknowledge that this may not be true, and that the law may have to change for the new challenges of AI and ADM.[92] However, given the scope of this work, we will proceed within the bounds of the assumption that the law is sufficient for now. The primary sources considered for this work are administrative law and judicial assessments of disparate impact in substantive equality cases. Specifically for administrative law, we narrow the scope further as explained in the section that immediately follows.

1.5.1 Narrowing the Scope of Administrative Law

In administrative law, the principle of procedural fairness ensures that administrative decisions adhere to procedures mandated in legislation or common law according to the theory that "the substance of a decision is more likely to be fair if the procedure through which that decision was made has

---

Impact Assessment] AIA in an accessible format and in both official languages on the Open Government Portal." At the time of writing, ten completed Algorithmic Impact Assessments were posted to the Open Government Portal at: https://search.open.canada.ca/opendata/?search_text=algorithmic+impact+assessment.

[91] See, e.g., Government of Canada, 'Responsible Use of Artificial Intelligence (AI): Exploring the Future of Responsible AI in Government' (2021) <https://www.canada.ca/en/government/system/digital-government/digital-government-innovations/responsible-use-ai.html>. See also UK Secretary of State for Digital Culture Media and Sport by Command of Her Majesty, 'National AI Strategy' (2021) <https://www.gov.uk/government/publications/national-ai-strategy> 40–48; David Freeman Engstrom and others, 'Government by Algorithm: Artificial Intelligence in Federal Administrative Agencies' (2020) <https://www-cdn.law.stanford.edu/wp-content/uploads/2020/02/ACUS-AI-Report.pdf> 21–69.

[92] See, e.g., Teresa Scassa, 'Administrative Law and the Governance of Automated Decision-Making' (2022) <https://www.youtube.com/watch?v=sn9AErX6ds0> discussed at 50–54 minutes.

been just."[93] The duty of fairness is required for administrative decisions that impact the "rights, privileges or interests of an individual."[94] Administrative bodies are not always required to provide reasons for their decisions. They may be required to do so if this is explicitly called for in the enabling statute, if the enabling statute includes a right of appeal, or based on the level of impact of the decision on the individual.[95] If a duty of fairness were not owed, or reasons for an administrative decision were not required, then the administrative decision being made would likely be of little consequence and the motivation for developing standards for algorithmic bias would be diminished. Therefore, the scope of the standards we are seeking is for the case where a duty of fairness is owed and a reason is required for the decision.

Whether or not the administrative body has complied with the obligation to provide a reason when required to do so is a question of procedural fairness in judicial review, while the quality of the reasons themselves is a matter of substantive review.[96] Procedural fairness includes, for example, ensuring that those impacted by administrative decisions have participatory rights such as the right to be notified about a decision made about them, the right to appeal or contest the decision, and that the administrative proceeding be an "impartial, and open process, appropriate to the statutory, institutional, and social context of the decision."[97] Procedural fairness is relevant to ML-based ADM systems, like any other administrative decision-making process. Research addressing how procedural fairness applies to ADM systems is already burgeoning and we do not attempt to summarize it here.[98] Rather, we focus on the substantive aspects of reasons, i.e., the quality of the reasons themselves. How courts approach and evaluate the quality of the reasons will inform the operational standards we propose here. While it is impossible to completely separate procedural fairness considerations completely from substantive review, our focus here is on the latter.

---

[93] Government of Canada, 'Citizenship: Natural Justice and Procedural Fairness' (2015) <https://www.canada.ca/en/immigration-refugees-citizenship/corporate/publications-manuals/operational-bulletins-manuals/canadian-citizenship/admininistration/decisions/natural-justice-procedural-fairness.html>.

[94] *Cardinal v. Director of Kent Institution* [1985] 2 SCR 643 at para 14.

[95] *Baker v. Minister of Citizenship and Immigration* (n 25) at para 43 as cited in Evan Fox-Decent and Alexander Pless, 'The Charter and Administrative Law Part I: Procedural Fairness' in Colleen M Flood and Lorne Sossin (eds), *Administrative Law in Context* (Third, Emond Montgomery Publications Limited 2018) 245.

[96] Fox-Decent and Pless (n 95) 246.

[97] *Baker v. Minister of Citizenship and Immigration* (n 39) 841

[98] See, e.g., Jennifer Cobbe, 'Administrative Law and the Machines of Government: Judicial Review of Automated Public-Sector Decision-Making' (2019) 39 Legal Studies 636; Scassa (n 60); Daly (n 88).

Before proceeding, we will provide two more elements of context necessary to this thesis in the next section: ADM in the context of soft law, and the status of soft law in judicial review.

1.5.2 Soft Law and Its Status in Judicial Review

Where ML is used to assist in making discretionary decisions, it typically means that a prediction has been generated for consideration by the decision-maker. ML predictions provide various types of information such as the likelihood of an event occurring; the likelihood that an individual would perform an action; a ranked estimation of need for services — conceivably any information derived from data. The quality of that prediction is shaped before it gets to the decision-maker, by the processes used in the design and development of the ML algorithm itself. The standards we propose for these processes would — if implemented by an administrative body — be considered elements of soft law as described in Section 1.2. Given that we are working within the premise that legal principles and precedent should inform soft-law standards, the reader might ask the related question as to whether soft law is subject to judicial review. The answer to this question for substantive review of an administrative decision is straightforward: yes, courts can and do evaluate the soft law used by the decision-maker.[99]

The answer is less clear with respect to a *Charter* analysis of soft law in judicial review. In their 2005 study, Pottie and Sossin found an inconsistent record — courts have, in some cases, extended their *Charter* analysis to include an administrative body's soft-law instruments, and in other cases, have declined to do so.[100] In reviewing the detailed accounts of the cases that make up their study findings, in only one case was there a wholesale rejection of *Charter* review of soft law due to the extensiveness of the material that the court would have to review.[101] Rather, the inconsistency noted by Pottie and Sossin most often stemmed from very particular legal interpretations in specific cases, or from the fact that the reviewing court was more interested in the effect of the soft law than the intricacies of it itself.[102] In his earlier work on

---

[99] Green (n 44) 334
[100] Laura Pottie and Lorne Sossin, 'Demystifying the Boundaries of Public Law: Policy, Discretion, and Social Welfare.' (2005) 38 U.B.C Law Review 147. See detailed analysis at 165–175 for reasons given by the courts for their decision to review or not to review soft law.
[101] Ibid. 172
[102] Ibid. 162–175

soft law, Sossin countered this, explaining that reviewing only the outcomes of individual challenges diminishes the likelihood that the problematic patterns in the soft-law policies and practices that created the problem in the first place will be corrected.[103] Taking this and other factors into account, Pottie and Sossin made a strong argument that the scope of *Charter* analysis in judicial review should include soft law when it meaningfully impacts the quality and substance of the resulting administrative decisions — which is relevant to our work here.[104] The authors explain that if administrative bodies *expect* to have soft law included in judicial review, it will drive them to develop soft law that takes *Charter* rights into account at the point of design, resulting in soft law that is more clearly articulated and has been vetted for compliance before being put into use.[105] Pottie and Sossin believe this will result in more fair and reasonable outcomes in administrative decision-making overall,[106] an approach with which our work is completely aligned.

1.6 METHODOLOGY

The central question to be addressed in this work is:

> In the context of the Directive, what standards can be derived from legal principles and precedent for the control of algorithmic bias in ML in order to mitigate disparate impact in administrative decisions?

The standards proposed span three dimensions of control: mitigating the creation of biased predictions; evaluating predictions for the influence of algorithmic bias; and, measuring disparity. Taken together, these standards provide a framework that agencies using ADM can leverage to mitigate disparate impact in administrative decisions. What precisely qualifies as a "standard" in the scope of this work? In the broad definition of standards provided earlier in Section 1.1 (footnote 22), the term standard could describe something as broad as a recommended practice, or could be as specific as a technical criterion or threshold. Technical standards are necessarily specific to a particular use case or industry sector application. It would be impossible to anticipate all the sectors and use cases for ADM in federal agencies, and

---

[103] Sossin (n 46) 480
[104] Pottie and Sossin (n 100) 179
[105] Ibid.
[106] Ibid. 187

as such the standards we propose will be stated generically — and thus may appear to the reader to be types or categories of standards. This is by design, and in Chapter 4, where the implementation of standards is discussed, we elaborate on how these generic standards can be adapted and made specific to a given policy and decision-making context.

Three additional scoping decisions are made in this work. First, recall the definition of ADM provided in the Directive: a "technology that *either assists or replaces* the judgement of human decision-makers."[107] Scholars have raised questions about the applicability of administrative law, which is concerned with the actions of human decision-makers, to the domain of ML-based ADM where the decision-maker could be the ADM system itself.[108] We consider only the use of ADM to assist human administrative decision-makers in making discretionary administrative decisions, and will not address the scenario of ADM replacing human decision-makers. Second, recall the previously discussed factors that contribute to algorithmic bias: societal; human; and statistical and computational. We consider only statistical and computational sources of algorithmic bias. Third, the standards we develop will not be an exhaustive set — they will be an illustrative set to prove the feasibility of deriving standards based on legal principles and precedent.

This work will proceed as follows. In Chapter 2, we examine the principles of administrative law, and in particular reasonableness review, in order to derive standards for the first two of the three dimensions: namely standards to mitigate the creation of biased predictions, and standards to evaluate predictions for the influence of algorithmic bias. In Chapter 3, we examine the SCC's test to prove *prima facie* discrimination, and how the measurement of disparity is at the heart of the *Charter* guarantee of substantive equality. We then trace the policy and legal history related to the measurement of disparity, synthesizing this background in order to propose standards for the third dimension of the control of algorithmic bias — the measurement of disparity.

In Chapter 4, we consolidate all the proposed standards into one overall framework, discuss key features of the framework, how the proposed standards relate to each other, and recommendations for agencies wishing to adopt them. In Chapter 5, we provide conclusions and areas for further research.

---

[107] Government of Canada Treasury Board Secretariat, 'Directive on Automated Decision-Making' (n 1). Appendix A: Definitions (emphasis added).

[108] See, e.g., Scassa (n 60). See also: Raso (n 6). Note however that Cobbe neutralizes these concerns, arguing that regardless of whether algorithms contributed to, or made the decision, common law will hold that humans within the government bodies remain accountable: "an unlawful decision made by or with the assistance of ADM should be dealt with by reviewers as it would be had a similarly unlawful decision been taken by a human" (see: Cobbe (n 98) 639–640).

Administrative Law and Standards for the Control of Algorithmic Bias

2

The premise for this chapter is that an understanding of administrative law principles, combined with a backward-looking understanding of how courts review and determine whether administrative decisions are reasonable, helps to inform forward-looking standards for the control of algorithmic bias in administrative decision-making. Material covered in this chapter spans both legal topics and ML topics, and the integration of the two. The standards proposed in this chapter span the first two dimensions of the control of algorithmic bias: standards to mitigate the creation of biased predictions, and standards for the evaluation of predictions for the influence of algorithmic bias. Throughout this chapter, we clarify the difference between procedural fairness in administrative law, and procedures to improve the quality of a prediction which are substantive concerns, and for which we are proposing standards. This chapter is organized as follows.

In Section 2.1, we review three foundational principles of administrative law (transparency, deference, and proportionality), articulating how automated decision-making engages these principles. In this section, we also describe the role of soft law in the administrative context, and define standards as soft law. In Section 2.2, we discuss and position the principles of reasonableness review within the culture of justification, and then outline an administrative decision-making scenario to be used throughout the remainder of the chapter to illustrate proposed standards to control algorithmic bias. In

DOI: 10.1201/b23364-2

Section 2.3, we propose and justify seven distinct standards to mitigate the creation of algorithmic bias in predictions.

In Section 2.4, we turn to standards oriented toward the evaluation of predictions for the influence of algorithmic bias. we begin by interrogating the concept of accuracy in predictions and inferences in detail — drawing from privacy law in Canada and the work of privacy scholars in Europe. This interrogation results in the proposal of standards for uncertainty. The chapter concludes with a discussion of the importance of individual fairness in the administrative context, and corresponding proposed standards. All proposed standards are consolidated in tabular format at the conclusion of the chapter.

2.1 FOUNDATIONAL PRINCIPLES: TRANSPARENCY, DEFERENCE AND PROPORTIONALITY

2.1.1 Transparency

In substantive review, the question the court is faced with is whether the decision in question was valid.[109] Courts evaluate administrative decisions according to a presumed reasonableness standard of review.[110] The SCC provided guidance on what constitutes "reasonableness" in the 2008 case of *Dunsmuir v. New Brunswick*:

> In judicial review, reasonableness is concerned mostly with the existence of **justification, transparency, and intelligibility** within the decision-making process. But it is also concerned with whether the decision falls

---

[109] Sossin and Lawrence (n 36) 124.

[110] Following a series of cases known as the *Administrative Law Trilogy*, in 2019 the Supreme Court of Canada (SCC) established two standards of substantive review for administrative decisions: correctness and reasonableness. The correctness standard of review means that there is one right answer. Courts use the correctness standard of review to evaluate primarily jurisdictional aspects of an administrative decision, and whether the administrative decision adheres to principles of the "rule of law." However, reasonableness is the *presumptive* standard of review for administrative decisions, except those meeting the specific requirements of correctness mentioned above. See: Supreme Court of Canada, 'Case Law in Brief: The Standard of Review (Taken from Vavilov in the "Administrative Law Trilogy")' (2019) <https://www.scc-csc.ca/case-dossier/cb/2019/37748-37896-37897-eng.pdf>.

within a range of possible, acceptable **outcomes** which are defensible in respect of the facts and law.[111]

Wildeman remarks that *Dunsmuir*'s elaboration of reasonableness integrates both procedural (i.e., reference to transparency) and substantive (i.e., reference to justification) aspects of judicial review inquiry.[112] Much has been written about the need for transparency in the context of algorithmic decision-making,[113] and we address the topic here to capture additional assumptions. Transparency has been identified among the top emerging principles for self-regulation of AI.[114] It features prominently in the EU AIA which makes transparency mandatory for all AI systems,[115] and a commitment to transparency is emphasized in the Preamble to the Directive. However, the word "transparency" is used to describe different types of obligations, and transparency in one context is not the same as transparency in another. In *Dunsmuir* as in the Directive, transparency refers to a guiding principle in government conduct,[116] which enables reason-giving. In contrast, in the EU AIA, transparency refers to the property of an AI system that renders its functioning and outputs interpretable.[117] In their study of the role of transparency in the use of algorithms for US administrative decision-making, Coglianese and Lehr contrast "fishbowl transparency" which discloses what actions and policies that the government is undertaking with ADM, with "reasoned transparency" which provides the rational basis for the decision the government is taking.[118] Due to the opacity of many algorithms, the authors explain that "machine learning presents its most distinctive challenge

---

[111] *Dunsmuir v. New Brunswick* [2008] 1 SCR 190, 220–221 (hereinafter "*Dunsmuir*") (emphasis added)

[112] Sheila Wildeman, 'Making Sense of Reasonablenss' in Colleen M Flood and Lorne Sossin (eds), *Administrative Law in Context* (Third, Emond Montgomery Publications Limited 2018) 463.

[113] See, e.g., Michele Finck, 'Automated Decision-Making and Administrative Law' in Peter Cane and others (eds), *Oxford Handbook of Comparative Administrative Law* (Oxford University Press 2020). See also: Alan FT Winfield and others, 'IEEE P7001: A Proposed Standard on Transparency' (2021) 8 Frontiers in Robotics and AI <https://www.frontiersin.org/articles/10.3389/frobt.2021.665729/full>.

[114] Anna Jobin, Marcello Ienca and Effy Vayena, 'The Global Landscape of AI Ethics Guidelines' (2019) 1 Nature Machine Intelligence 389 <http://www.nature.com/articles/s42256-019-0088-2> 1.

[115] European Commission (n 14) 7.

[116] Government of Canada, 'Transparency - ESDC' (2020) <https://www.canada.ca/en/employment-social-development/corporate/transparency.html>.

[117] European Commission (n 14). Chapter 2 Article 13(1).

[118] Cary Coglianese and David Lehr, 'TRANSPARENCY AND ALGORITHMIC GOVERNANCE' (2019) 71 Administrative Law Review 1, 13–14

to reasoned transparency, not fishbowl transparency,"[119] although without the latter it is difficult to achieve the former. For this work, we do not address transparency as a property of AI systems. We assume fishbowl transparency is in place and will limit our inquiry to the obligation for reasoned transparency wherein decision-makers must show how the reasons and their reasoning process led to the decision.

2.1.2 Deference

Courts approach review of administrative reasoning from a position of "deference as respect,"[120] which means that courts consider the specialized expertise and experience that administrative bodies have in the domain over which they preside — including technical expertise, expertise in relevant statutory interpretation and experience accumulated over time. This expertise informs the soft-law instruments that administrative bodies use to guide their decisions. Standards for algorithmic bias would contribute to an administrative body's soft law, and as described in Section 1.5.2 courts do consider the content of soft law in their analysis of reasonableness. In *Baker*, it was explained that: "important weight must be given [in judicial review] to the choice of procedures made by the agency itself and its institutional constraints."[121] The corollary is that courts expect that the agency has followed the procedures it has established to make a decision, as a matter of procedural fairness.[122]

Administrative bodies using ML-based ADM, and seeking deference from reviewing courts, therefore must fulfil several obligations. First, the administrative body must have access to sufficient expertise in ML to develop their own standards and/or to assess external standards, and to implement standards for algorithmic bias in their specific decision-making context. Coglianese describes having sufficient expertise as an important "precondition for use" of ML for administrative agencies.[123] While it may seem an obvious point, skills shortages in ML — especially in understanding and implementing practical approaches to the control of algorithmic bias — are a very real challenge for all organizations, government, and otherwise

---

[119] Ibid. 14.
[120] Liston (n 43) 162.
[121] *Baker v. Minister of Citizenship and Immigration* (n 39) 840.
[122] Ibid. 839.
[123] Cary Coglianese, 'A Framework for Governmental Use of Machine Learning' (2020) <https://www.acus.gov/sites/default/files/documents/Coglianese ACUS Final Report w Cover Page.pdf> 66.

around the world.[124] Second, it's not enough just to implement standards, but their use must be monitored for compliance, and records kept.[125] To this end, Cobbe, Lee, and Singh have proposed a wholistic and practical "reviewability" framework for ADM with specific requirements at each step of the ML lifecycle derived from English law in administrative decision-making.[126]

Third, decision-makers need to ensure that the soft-law standards they have developed and implemented effectively serve the relevant policy or statutory objective at hand. While there is not a lot of research on soft law in practice in Canada, we briefly highlight the findings and implications from three studies here to illustrate challenges in implementation.

In their 2005 analysis, Pottie and Sossin interviewed decision-makers in British Columbia, Ontario, Nunavut, and Prince Edward Island who participated in the decision-making process for welfare eligibility, or who participated in challenges to welfare eligibility decisions. Welfare eligibility is a discretionary decision, in a setting in which a high volume of such decisions are required of a typically understaffed and under-supervised set of front-line workers.[127] In this setting, Pottie and Sossin found that "policy guidelines serve as the accessible and comprehensive source to which decision-makers look for answers."[128] However, Pottie and Sossin further uncovered that guidelines were often interpreted by front-line workers not as instruments to be used in support of making a contextually sensitive decision, but rather as hard and fast rules[129] — the very opposite of what discretionary decision-making is designed to be.

Cumming and Caragata also studied discretionary decision-making in a social welfare setting, finding vast differences in organizational culture and practices across welfare offices in Ontario, despite being subject to the same legislatively enacted policies across those offices. The authors concluded that an ideology of "rationing" welfare benefits, targeting single mothers in

---

[124] Ibid. 40. See also Coglianese and Lehr (n 118). 20. A recent white paper for the Stanford Institute for Human-Centered Artificial Intelligence and the Stanford Regulation, Evaluation, and Governance Lab, identifies a "serious resource shortage" as the root of many of the implementation challenges associated with the US government's AI Strategy (see: Christie Lawrence, Isaac Cui, and Daniel E Ho, 'Implementation Challenges to Three Pillars of America's AI Strategy' (2022) <https://hai.stanford.edu/sites/default/files/2022-12/HAIRegLab White Paper - Implementation Challenges to Three Pillars of America's AI Strategy.pdf> 5).

[125] Regarding record keeping, see: Daly (n 88) 22–23.

[126] Jennifer Cobbe, Michelle Seng Ah Lee and Jatinder Singh, 'Reviewable Automated Decision-Making', *Proceedings of the 2021 ACM Conference on Fairness, Accountability, and Transparency* (ACM 2021) <https://dl.acm.org/doi/10.1145/3442188.3445921>.

[127] Pottie and Sossin (n 100) 147.

[128] Ibid. 154.

[129] Ibid. 155.

particular, had arisen in some offices and reflected notions of "conditionality and disentitlement,"[130] contrary to the policies which mandated an assessment of need as the basis for decision-making. Soft law in the form of skewed policy interpretation, coupled with administrative culture, had negatively impacted these particular claimants' access to supplemental welfare benefits — and potentially implicated rights interferences by singling out particular group(s).

In her recent study of front-line decision-makers administering the Ontario Works social assistance program, Raso illustrated how reasons for administrative decisions, and client outcomes arising from those decisions, were shaped not only by institutional pressures and practices, but also by the limitations of the technological systems used by front-line decision-makers. For example, Raso discovered instances where the design and workflow parameters of the technological systems limited decision-makers' reasoning processes in ways contrary to legislative intent, effectively imposing a questionable soft-law regime on decision-makers and influencing substantive outcomes for clients of the Ontario Works program.[131] Raso's study vividly illustrates that it is the interaction between systems (that encode soft law, whether by design or not) and decision-makers that determines decisions and outcomes.

These studies prompt questions about the quality of soft law, and how it is used in day-to-day discretionary decision-making. Is it clear enough? Is the scope for allowable interpretation too broad or too narrow? How are decision-makers trained, do they have sufficient time and resources to fulfil their mandates? How are decisions monitored for coherence with the original policy or legislative intent? The people, practices, and technological systems through which soft law is implemented, not only the content of the soft law itself, impact both how effective that soft law will be at achieving its aims, as well as how a court might look upon that soft law in judicial review. In the context of our work, this means that developing and implementing standards is not enough on its own for judicial deference: standards must be supported by skilled agency teams and decision-makers, well-designed technological systems, and an operating culture and practice that taken together reinforce the objective of mitigating disparate impact.

---

[130] Sara Cumming and Lea Caragata, 'Rationing "Rights": Supplementary Welfare Benefits and Lone Moms' (2011) 12 Critical Social Work 82 < https://ojs.uwindsor.ca/index.php/csw/article/view/5844>.

[131] Jennifer Raso, 'Unity in the Eye of the Beholder? Reasons for Decision in Theory and Practice in the Ontario Works Program' (2019) 70 University of Toronto Law Journal 1, 22–23.

2.1.3 Proportionality

The principle of proportionality applies both to procedural fairness as well as to substantive review. A proportional approach to procedural fairness was elaborated in *Baker*: "The duty of procedural fairness is flexible and variable and depends on an appreciation of the context of the particular statute and the rights affected."[132] In other words, the greater the impact of the decision on the claimant, the greater the required duty of procedural fairness. The weight that should be allotted to *Charter* rights in judicial review of administrative decisions is also based on proportionality. In *Doré v. Barreau du Québec*, the SCC developed a balancing test of reasonableness adapted to discretionary decisions:

> In the *Charter* context, the reasonableness analysis is one that centres on proportionality, that is, on ensuring that the decision interferes with the relevant *Charter* guarantee no more than is necessary given the statutory objectives. If the decision is disproportionately impairing of the guarantee, it is unreasonable.[133]

Justice Abella further wrote that decision-makers should protect *Charter* rights in the context of the statutory objective that grants the decision-maker discretionary powers.[134] Unless explicitly controlled and mitigated, the potential for algorithmic bias and disparate impact (contrary to the *Charter* guarantee of substantive equality) *always* exists when ML algorithms are used to provide information to assist decision-makers. Therefore, agencies must *always* adopt measures to measure, mitigate and control algorithmic bias and the outcome of disparate impact — the degree to which is determined by the statutory objective. In proposing standards in this chapter, we do so generically given that they are not specific to any particular decision. However, putting these proposed standards into practice would require that a proportional approach be applied, which we address in Chapter 4.

2.2 REASONABLENESS REVIEW

The starting point for this work is understanding reasons as central to the "culture of justification," that developed after the *Charter* was enacted, as described by Justice Beverly McLachlin: "Where a society is marked by a

---

[132] *Baker v. Minister of Citizenship and Immigration* (n 39) 819.
[133] *Doré v. Barreau du Québec* [2012] 1 SCR 395, 398.
[134] Ibid. 426.

culture of justification, an exercise of public power is only appropriate where it can be justified to citizens in terms of *rationality and fairness.*"[135] Reasons are the mechanism for this justification. Reasons are how decision-makers communicate the factors that were considered in coming to a decision to those impacted by that decision. Sound reasons intuitively imply that the decision-making process has been rational and fair, and Daly explains further that:

> Where reasons are absent or inadequate, an individual may be able to point to arbitrariness, inconsistency with previous policy, breach of legitimate expectation and other indicia or badges of unreasonableness which would justify a court in striking down the decision.[136]

What we are concerned with in this work is how decision-makers justify their reasons, when ML-based algorithms have been used to provide information to assist decision-makers. And our premise is that if justification is enabled using standards, better and more fair decisions — mitigated for disparate impact — will result.

The SCC's broad description of reasonableness has resulted in inconsistency in the way it has been interpreted in judicial review post-*Dunsmuir*.[137] Daly attributes this inconsistency to a lingering traditional view of administrative decision-making that centred upon administrative authority, and that did not reflect the contemporary culture of justification.[138] The SCC's 2019 majority decision in *Canada (Minister of Citizenship and Immigration) v. Vavilov* clarified what constitutes a reasonable administrative decision and reset expectations for decision-makers in terms of the importance and means of justifying their decisions. In Daly's analysis of *Vavilov*, he distils the clarifications of reasonableness provided by the SCC as placing a renewed emphasis on four dimensions of justification: reasoned decision-making, responsiveness, demonstrated expertise, and contextualism.[139] In brief, "reasoned decision-making" means that justification for an administrative decision must be meaningful *to the individual impacted by the decision* and not a generic justification; "responsiveness" "places the individual at the centre

---

[135] Beverly McLachlin, 'The Roles of Administrative Tribunals and Courts in Maintaining the Rule of Law' (1999) 12 Canadian Journal of Administrative Law & Practice 171, 174 (emphasis is original).

[136] Daly (n 88) 21.

[137] Wildeman (n 112) 499–500.

[138] Paul Daly, 'Vavilov and the Culture of Justification in Contemporary Administrative Law' (2021) 100 The Supreme Court Law Review: Osgoode's Annual Constitutional Cases Conference 279, 281.

[139] Ibid. 282–290.

of the reason-giving process"[140] and requires decision-makers to consider the impact of the decision to the individual as part of the reasoning process; "demonstrated expertise" means that the decision-maker's expertise should not be accepted as a given, but *evidence* provided as to how that expertise has been used in the decision-making process; and, "contextualism" avoids cookie-cutter reasons for decisions, requiring decision-makers to link their reasons with the specific context at hand. Daly's analysis describes modern judicial expectations of the conduct of administrative decision-makers.

Looking at reasonableness from the point of view of precedent, scholars have proposed a consolidated set of "indicia of unreasonableness" — qualities of administrative decisions that have been seen to recur across court challenges and that could serve to flag courts and administrative decision-makers to potential problems with the substance of decisions.[141] Wildeman's summary of these indicia include the following: "unintelligibility" in the decision-making process; unexplained "inconsistency" in the decision-making process; lack of a "reasonable basis in the evidence"; "unreasonable interpretations or applications of law"; "lack of reasonable support in the legislative context"; "failure to consider a relevant factor"; "consideration of an irrelevant factor"; and "disproportionality" in the limitation of a *Charter* right.[142] Other factors that courts consider when assessing reasons for an administrative decision include, for example, whether there is a reasonable apprehension of individual or institutional bias in the decision-making process,[143] and whether the facts and evidence used by the government body to arrive at their decision "logically connect" to the decision.[144] These indicia of unreasonableness point to common problems identified by prior judicial review, a backward look at things that have gone wrong. Taken together, Daly's four dimensions of justification and the indicia of unreasonableness help to inform standards.

We offer several observations before proceeding. First, the indicia of unreasonableness are not completely independent of each other, especially in the context of algorithmic bias. One indication often suggests another and as such, the indicia tend to be clustered, for example: if there is no reasonable basis in the evidence, then the facts or evidence used to arrive at the decision cannot logically connect to the decision; or, if an irrelevant factor was

---

[140] Ibid. 284.

[141] Wildeman (n 112) 499.

[142] Ibid. 501–504.

[143] Laverne Jacobs, 'The Dynamics of Independence, Impartiality, and Bias in the Canadian Administrative State' in Colleen M Flood and Lorne Sossin (eds), *Administrative Law in Context* (Third, Emond Montgomery Publications Limited 2018) 280.

[144] Raso (n 6) 197.

considered, then there is no reasonable basis in the evidence and/or there was unintelligibility in the decision-making process. For the purpose of proposing standards, it is not important to try to separate the indicia, it is enough to make a connection between algorithmic bias and one or more indicia.

Second, we will not touch upon all the indicia — the five that will recur here are: unintelligibility in the decision-making process; lack of connection between the facts or evidence used to arrive at the decision, and the decision itself; reasonable basis in evidence; consideration of an irrelevant factor; and, unexplained inconsistency in the decision-making process.

Third, we are not providing an exhaustive analysis in this chapter — this analysis will instead be illustrative across some of the most important factors that contribute to the creation of algorithmic bias. Fourth, plain language meanings of the indicia are assumed. For example, Wildeman uses unintelligibility to describe circumstances in which the logic of the decision-maker's reasoning is unclear, incomplete, or lacking in logical coherence.[145] While it is true that in judicial review courts would apply very precise definitions of the indicia of unreasonableness and would draw upon relevant precedent to do so, for our purposes here, plain language meanings of the indicia are sufficient. Finally, we will occasionally draw from social science research methodologies where relevant to help explain algorithmic bias, because these proven methods also suggest standards for the control of algorithmic bias.

Algorithmic bias can result from the procedures used to design and build the algorithm. We emphasize again that procedures used to control algorithmic bias are not to be confused with the principle of procedural fairness in administrative law. The procedures we propose here shape substantive aspects of the algorithms and are captured in the agency's soft law. Each standard addresses *a single facet of the same multi-faceted question*: Can the use of the algorithm be justified as rational and fair, to those impacted by it?

2.2.1 Illustrative Scenario

Throughout this discussion, we reference a simple, hypothetical scenario to illustrate how ML could be used by an administrative decision-maker, and within which to situate controls for algorithmic bias. In this scenario, a federal economic development agency (the Agency) is devising a program to provide start-up funding for new businesses in a particular geographic area. This new program is authorized by legislation that indicates that the Agency intends to use ML-based predictions to assist in making equitable

---

[145] Wildeman (n 112) 501.

administrative decisions about where to allocate the funding. The Agency notes the Directive's policy requirements; however, it has not yet put in place processes to establish compliance with these requirements and is interested in understanding how to operationalize controls for algorithmic bias.

In prior funding programs the Agency has deployed, some business owners used funds they received fraudulently. Once the fraud was discovered, the Agency's investigators anecdotally observed patterns in these business owners' original application responses that they considered to be an early warning that fraud could occur. For example, some business owners had misreported their credit scores or had exaggerated their prior business experience. The Agency has limited funds to allocate, and in moving forward with this new program wants to ensure that this time none of their funding is used fraudulently. Due to the high volume of applications, the agency plans to use supervised ML[146] on the historical data from the prior funding program, to build a model that predicts whether an applicant has potentially committed fraud. Then new applications will be assessed using the ML model and a prediction is to be computed which the Agency terms a "risk score" — the likelihood that the new application is being made by an individual with a proclivity to fraudulent use of funds based on their application responses.[147] The *prediction* is the ML statistical computation. Labelling the prediction as a "risk score" is the *inference* being made by the Agency as to the meaning of the prediction. The risk score will be provided to the decision-maker to assist in determining whether the application should be approved for funding. The risk score is just one piece of information the decision-maker will use to render their decision.

At this stage, the Agency has made several implicit assumptions in their development and use of ML predictions to assist in their decision-making. These assumptions identify points in the ML lifecycle where controls for algorithmic bias are required — areas that if left ungoverned could expose the agency to the potential of making decisions that are misinformed by the ML, that could be deemed unreasonable in judicial review, or that could lead

---

[146] Supervised learning is defined as "learning a function from a training set," and "the function learned is called a model of the underlying system generating that data." (see: Richard E Neapolitan and Xia Jiang, *Artificial Intelligence: With an Introduction to Machine Learning*, vol 1 (2nd edn, CRC Press 2018) 89–90). The supervised learning described in the illustrative scenario is regression modelling.

[147] While the example presented here is a simplified one of regression modelling, the standards that we illustrate using this example apply equally in the context of more complex ML algorithms. Further, doing so is consistent with the Directive's definition of automated decision systems spans both simple and complex algorithmic processes. See: Government of Canada Treasury Board Secretariat, 'Directive on Automated Decision-Making' (n 1). Appendix A — Definitions.

to discriminatory outcomes in violation of *Charter* guarantees. In this chapter, we investigate each of these assumptions, propose relevant standards to mitigate the creation of algorithmic bias, and justify these standards based on administrative law. We further note that in the discussion that follows, the Agency conduct is illustrative, and in no way reflects specifically on any real, past, or anticipated conduct of any Agency of the federal government of Canada.

2.3 STANDARDS TO MITIGATE THE CREATION OF BIASED PREDICTIONS

2.3.1 Construct Validity

Suppose the application for funding was highly simplified, inquiring only about the applicant's current credit score and declared earnings on their most recent tax return, and this was the only information the Agency used to design and build the risk score. The implicit assumption being made is that the underlying human characteristics measured by current credit score and earnings are truly related to the human characteristics underlying the likelihood to commit future fraudulent behaviour. This design assumption is the *construct* that the Agency has implicitly adopted that describes human behaviour. The Agency is also implicitly assuming that the construct holds steady across the different time periods and circumstances separating the prior funding program and the current.

Constructs about human behaviour as described in this example are almost always unobservable, relying instead on theories and logical reasoning rather than provable causality.[148] While construct validity — having a valid basis upon which to conclude that a system of relationships reflects an underlying truth — has been central to traditional research methodology in social sciences, there has been far less of this methodological rigour in the rise of ML methods, which have been described as "atheoretical,"[149] where the data is left to speak for itself. An atheoretical approach has contributed to the widespread outcomes of algorithmic bias described in Chapter 1, where

---

[148] Babbie (n 64) 192.

[149] Ives C Passos and others, 'Machine Learning and Big Data Analytics in Bipolar Disorder: A Position Paper from the International Society for Bipolar Disorders Big Data Task Force' (2019) 21 Bipolar disorders 582, 583.

true relationships are distorted and the resulting predictions are without merit. Awareness of the relationship between *construct validity* and algorithmic bias has grown in recent years, and the lack thereof is now well-understood as a source of algorithmic bias.[150] Problems with construct validity relate to at least two of the indicia of unreasonableness: unintelligibility and the consideration of an irrelevant factor. Lacking a valid construct, the Agency could struggle to justify their reasoning for the design of the risk score as part of the overall decision-making scheme, implicating unintelligibility. And then having used the unjustified (and potentially biased) risk score to assist in decision-making, a reviewer could conclude that the decision-maker had considered an irrelevant factor. As such, agencies should establish standards for construct validity when using ML to assist decision-makers.

2.3.2 Representativeness of Input Data

In generating a predictive model using data from applicants in the prior program and then applying that model in the current program, the Agency is implicitly assuming that the data used to build the model is a *representative* sample of the population of applicants it is intending to describe. In social science methodologies, lack of representativeness of the data is known as sampling bias,[151] and its effects are well-understood to result in algorithmic bias in the ML context as well.[152] Ensuring that the ML model is based on representative data is necessary to control algorithmic bias. For example, if the Agency planned to use the model to build a risk score for *all* new applicants that could be men, women or non-binary, it would mean that the Agency couldn't use data solely from, say, applicants who identified as men to build the model. Doing so would likely incur algorithmic bias. To some readers this may seem obvious, a very basic step in the design of the ML system. However, lack of representativeness of data has been a significant problem in practice — with many more possible manifestations of it than the simple example provided[153] — often attributed to the fact that ML has simply been used on large amounts of data that are available versus according

---

[150] Schwartz and others (n 66). 15. See also extended discussion in: Sorelle A Friedler, Carlos Scheidegger, and Suresh Venkatasubramanian, 'On the (Im)Possibility of Fairness' 2016 <http://arxiv.org/abs/1609.07236>.

[151] Babbie (n 64) 132.

[152] Schwartz and others (n 66) 9.

[153] International Organization for Standardization (n 81) 10–13.

to good sampling practices.[154] The biased outcomes of facial recognition and language models are among some of the most prominent examples in the public eye.[155] If the data that the Agency used to build the model represented population "A" and the model based on that population was used to make inferences about proclivity for risk in population "B" that didn't share the characteristics of "A," then how would the risk scores be in any way relevant for decision-making purposes? A decision informed by a prediction based on non-representative data could be looked upon as unreasonable due to the consideration of an irrelevant factor. Both ISO[156] and NIST[157] identify non-representative sampling as a source of algorithmic bias in their standards. Writing for the Administrative Conference of the United States of America, Coglianese identifies the availability of representative data to be one of the three most important preconditions for the use of ML in administrative decision-making.[158] Thus, it is recommended that the Agency institute a standard for representativeness of input data.

2.3.3 Knowledge Limits

Even if construct validity has been established, and the data has been determined to be representative for the predictive task at hand, these assertions are typically valid at a point in time and for particular conditions in the algorithm's design phase. In the ML literature, "concept drift" describes how data and conditions change over time, and how attention must be paid to the degree to which such drift challenges the representativeness of data or renders the algorithm no longer suitable to the predictive task at hand.[159] In the US administrative context, Coglianese counsels agencies to put in place means to protect against harms arising from changes in external conditions and data representativeness over time, and from the use of algorithms

---

[154] Schwartz and others (n 66) 15.
[155] See, e.g., Sidney Perkowitz, 'The Bias in the Machine: Facial Recognition Technology and Racial Disparities' [2021] MIT Case Studies in Social and Ethical Responsibilities of Computing <https://mit-serc.pubpub.org/pub/bias-in-machine>; Paul Pu Liang and others, 'Towards Understanding and Mitigating Social Biases in Language Models' (2021) <http://arxiv.org/abs/2106.13219>. See alternate view with geopolitical implications: Stewart Baker, 'The Flawed Claims About Bias in Facial Recognition' (*Lawfare*, 2022) <https://www.lawfareblog.com/flawed-claims-about-bias-facial-recognition>.
[156] International Organization for Standardization (n 81) 11.
[157] Schwartz and others (n 66) Section 15–17.
[158] Coglianese (n 123) 68.
[159] See, e.g., Geoffrey I Webb and others, 'Characterizing Concept Drift' (2016) 30 Data Mining and Knowledge Discovery 964 <http://link.springer.com/10.1007/s10618-015-0448-4>.

in domains for which they were not intended.[160] NIST's proposed governance principle of "knowledge limits" can be applied to these challenges.[161] Knowledge limits require that the conditions under which the algorithm will produce reliable and accurate results is declared.

In the illustrative scenario, say that the amount of funding available successful applicants to the economic development program increased or decreased significantly over time, attracting a very different type of applicant to the funding program across different time periods. The model based on the initial distribution of funding amounts and the construct upon which it relied may no longer be valid, i.e., it is conceivable that the amount of available funding changes the behavioural construct. Similarly, the data used to build the initial model may no longer be representative of the population of current applicants. These examples describe how concept drift could manifest in this scenario. Further, if applicant risk scores were shared with other federal agencies and used to extrapolate a general proclivity to fraud, this would be beyond the scope of knowledge limits unless the agencies involved had coordinated a validation method to prove the transferability of the risk score from one context to the other. Simply put, agencies must put in place procedures for monitoring for concept drift, and associated standards that mandate working within knowledge limits. While the actual monitoring would occur after the algorithms have been deployed, the monitoring standard itself and specific knowledge limits should be identified during the design of the algorithm.

Why would these standards be important to reason-giving and justification of administrative decisions? A blunt answer is that any reasonable person could conclude that using algorithms subject to concept drift or outside of a declared set of knowledge limits is baseless. How could such a practice be seen as reasonable, or be thought to lead to a justifiable decision, by a reviewing court? One might argue that an agency would never make such poor choices as using a model exhibiting concept drift or beyond declared knowledge limits. But how will the agency even know they are doing so if they are not monitoring their activity according to relevant standards? .

Further, monitoring algorithms for concept drift, and establishing and adhering to knowledge limits is a recommended practice by SDOs and ML authorities.[162] Agencies using ML to advise decision-makers should stay

---

[160] Coglianese (n 123) 68–69.

[161] P Jonathon Phillips and others, 'National Institute of Standards and Technology Interagency or Internal Report 8312: Four Principles of Explainable Artificial Intelligence' (2020) <https://nvlpubs.nist.gov/nistpubs/ir/2020/NIST.IR.8312-draft.pdf> 4.

[162] See overviews of monitoring requirements, inclusive of monitoring for concept drift in Schwartz and others (n 66). 42–43; see also integrated discussion of monitoring and drift in International Organization for Standardization (n 81). 20–21. For a technical discussion of

abreast of such evolving practices, and build them into the design and deployment of algorithms. We argue that doing so is part of the requirement for providing evidence of expertise according to Daly's third dimension of justification post-*Vavilov*. Agencies that demonstrate having and applying appropriate expertise to the decision-making process — including expertise applicable to modern, evolving techniques such as ML — will be better positioned for deference by a reviewing court, and their use of such expertise should lead to more reasonable and justified administrative decisions.

2.3.4 Measurement Validity in Model Inputs

Another implicit assumption made by the Agency in developing the risk score is that the measurement of the input variables (credit score and earnings) are adequate measures for each of the factors they are intended to capture. This assumption is what is referred to in social science as measurement validity, i.e., "the extent to which an empirical measure adequately reflects the real meaning of the concept under consideration."[163] In their discussion of algorithmic bias, NIST names measurement bias — i.e., where the assumption of measurement validity does not hold — as a contributor to algorithmic bias.[164] For example, take credit score in our illustrative scenario — a calculation designed to "predict the likelihood that individuals will pay their bills as agreed" based on numerous factors.[165] According to credit-scoring agencies, approximately 15% of an individual's credit score is determined by how long their credit accounts have been open, favouring those with long-held credit accounts[166] and disadvantaging others such as newcomers to Canada or those who simply choose not to use credit. What is the Agency attempting to measure with credit score? Is the method of calculation appropriate or is it introducing bias into the measurement process?

It is possible that for the Agency's purposes, credit score is a valid measure, and their assumption holds. It is also possible that credit score is a proxy for something else the Agency would like to measure, but the Agency chooses

---

monitoring for concept drift, see, e.g., Xianzhe Zhou and others, 'A Framework to Monitor Machine Learning Systems Using Concept Drift Detection' in Witold Abramowicz and Rafael Corchuelo (eds), *Lecture Notes in Business Information Processing* (22nd Inter, 2019) <http://link.springer.com/10.1007/978-3-030-20485-3_17>.

[163] Babbie (n 64) 191.

[164] Schwartz and others (n 66) 52.

[165] Equifax Inc., 'How Are Credit Scores Calculated?' (2022) <https://www.equifax.com/personal/education/credit/score/how-is-credit-score-calculated/>.

[166] Ibid.

to use credit-score data to approximate their desired measure because credit-score data is easily collected. Or, perhaps the Agency deliberately seeks a measure defined as credit score — the likelihood that individuals will pay their bills as agreed — but how it is calculated by credit-scoring agencies is unbeknownst to the Agency. Either way, in these examples, credit score is a *proxy* measure. In the former, it is a proxy for some other desired measure; in the latter case, it could be a proxy for years without a credit history. In both cases, there is the potential that the Agency's use of credit score will cause biased predictions of risk.

In the illustrative scenario above, the proxy characteristics of the input variable credit score are easily described, and so measurement validity (or the lack thereof) is easy to grasp. Similarly, the earlier discussion of construct validity in Section 2.2.2 was based on easily understood measures. In reality, the input variables in a machine learning exercise can be more complex, computed measures known as features. Feature engineering is a sophisticated task carried out by algorithm designers and developers, which can include the transformation and generation of new features from existing variables and features (through human assessment or through embedded computation and ML).[167] Features used in ML can, but do not always, have some directly accessible meaning. Whether due to embedded bias on the input variables that comprise the features, or the mathematical and statistical procedures used to engineer features, feature engineering is well-understood to be a potential source of algorithmic bias.[168]

A related question arises of whether input variables or features directly or indirectly implicate a ground of discrimination under the *Charter*. For example, what if the Agency had decided to use age as an input variable?[169] Using age to allocate funding (via the calculation of the risk score) could be interpreted as disparate treatment based on age,[170] and could result in disparate impact. The use of age would clearly have to be justified as reasonable and non-discriminatory. If the use of age as an input variable enabled the Agency to make deliberate efforts to correct historical imbalances according to section 15(2) of the *Charter*, then the justification might

---

[167] For a comprehensive discussion of feature engineering, see, e.g., Guozhu Dong and Huan Liu, *Feature Engineering for Machine Learning and Data Analytics* (CRC Press 2018).

[168] International Organization for Standardization (n 81) 12–13.

[169] The use of age is a simple, hypothetical example for illustration purposes. Note that legal consultations (which could identify the potential for the illustrated disparate treatment) are required by the Directive during the planning stages of the automated decision-making system. See: Omar Bitar, Benoit Deshaies and Dawn Hall, '3rd Review of the Treasury Board Directive on Automated Decision-Making' [2022] SSRN Electronic Journal <https://www.ssrn.com/abstract=4087546> 7.

[170] Kroll and others (n 86) 695.

stand. On the other hand, the Agency might choose to exclude age as an input variable altogether to avoid disparate impact and potentially discriminatory decisions — a controversial strategy known in the ML literature as "fairness by blindness."[171] However, the Agency would still need to be concerned about whether other input variables functioned as proxies for age (or race, sex, and other possible grounds for discrimination), indirectly leading to discriminatory outcomes.

Agencies seeking to minimize algorithmic bias must take measurement validity, and the adjacent question of whether model inputs are directly or indirectly grounds for discrimination, very seriously. It is intuitively obvious that problems with measurement validity resulting in algorithmic bias could cause reviewers to question whether the decision-makers had considered an irrelevant factor in coming to their decision and could make it difficult to justify a decision. And, using input variables that are, or mirror, grounds of discrimination without a well-founded justification could spark a *Charter* challenge. Standards must be put in place at the point of algorithm design to ensure appropriate inspection of input variables and features for measurement validity, which include assessing whether any of the input variables or features that contribute to the algorithm's predictions are explicitly or implicitly equivalent to a ground for discrimination according to the *Charter* section 15(1).

2.3.5 Measurement Validity in Output Variables

In the above discussion, the potential for introducing bias into the algorithm's predictions due to the use of proxy measures or features for model *inputs* was discussed. Additional problems occur when the target of prediction lacks measurement validity, i.e., where the target of prediction is itself a proxy. Corbett-Davies and others refer to this as "label bias," describing it as the "most serious obstacle facing fair machine learning."[172] Obermeyer and others illustrated label bias at work in their study of healthcare researchers who seek to predict individuals' future healthcare *needs* using models that predict

---

[171] Brian Christian, *The Alignment Problem* (W W Norton & Company Inc 2020). 65. Citing Moritz Hardt, author Brian Christian summarized the prevailing view that fairness by blindness is ineffective due in large part to proxies. See also: Solon Barocas and Andrew D Selbst, 'Big Data's Disparate Impact' (2016) 104 California law review 671.

[172] Sam Corbett-Davies and Sharad Goel, 'The Measure and Mismeasure of Fairness: A Critical Review of Fair Machine Learning' (2018) <http://arxiv.org/abs/1808.00023> 17.

their future healthcare *costs*, because cost data is more readily available.[173] Healthcare costs and healthcare needs are two different things, and the authors elaborate on the numerous problems with cost data — such as embedded racial inequities due to historical and structural lack of access to healthcare for some populations — which renders cost a proxy and a biased prediction of need. This manifestation of algorithmic bias resembles that discussed earlier regarding *input* proxy measures. However, the target of prediction in an ML algorithm additionally encodes the policy objective it was built for, serving as the mechanism by which a government policy is implemented.[174]

To illustrate this relationship to policy, consider Obermeyer and others' aforementioned model for healthcare needs, which is really predicting the proxy target of future healthcare costs. Suppose the model were embedded in an automated decision system that delivers government benefits according to a stated policy of equitable distribution of benefits at a given level of need. The mis-specification of the target variable (future cost vs. need) and the resulting bias in the predictions means that decisions will not be equitable in their effects. The decisions would be equalizing benefits based on future cost instead of need, thereby compromising the government policy implementation.

Proxy measures, whether relating to the input variables and features, or relating to the target of prediction, present significant challenges to be overcome by agencies seeking to use ML to assist in decision-making. Proxy measures *definitely* compromise measurement variability. In doing so they frustrate any attempt at a reasonable justification, potentially compromise the administrative policy for which ADM was devised, and open the door for reviewers to conclude that predictions leveraging proxy measures were irrelevant factors for decision-making.[175] It is very important that any agency using ML detect and mitigate the harmful effects of proxy variables, putting in place standards to inspect and verify measurement validity in the target of prediction, and ensuring that it is appropriate to the policy context at hand.

---

[173] Ziad Obermeyer and others, 'Algorithmic Bias Playbook' (2021) <https://www.chicagobooth.edu/research/center-for-applied-artificial-intelligence/research/algorithmic-bias/playbook> 2–3.

[174] The relationship between the algorithm and policy is described in various ways in the literature. Some authors discuss the "objective function"; see, e.g., Coglianese and Lehr (n 118) 7; Coglianese (n 123) 45, 67; David Freeman Engstrom and Daniel E Ho, 'Algorithmic Accountability in the Administrative State' (2020) 37 Yale journal on regulation 800, 833, 839; Yoan Hermstrüwer, 'Artificial Intelligence and Administrative Decisions Under Uncertainty', *Regulating Artificial Intelligence* (Springer International Publishing 2020), 207. Other authors descibe how policies are translated into the algorithm's properties; see, e.g., Kroll and others (n 86) 642, 696.

[175] Cobbe (n 98) 651

2.3.6 Accuracy of Input Data

Federal agency collection and use of personal data for an administrative purpose is subject to the requirements of the *Privacy Act* which states:

> A government institution shall take all reasonable steps to ensure that personal information that is used for an administrative purpose by the institution is as **accurate, up-to-date and complete as possible.**[176]

We assume for present purposes that the accuracy of personal data is easily established, and thus it is straightforward for agencies to comply with the accuracy principle of the *Privacy Act*.[177] However, what protections apply to other data an agency might be interested in, as input to a predictive algorithm, that is *not considered personal data* and thus not covered by the *Privacy Act*'s requirements? This question cannot be ignored because agencies may be legitimately interested in enriching their ML algorithms with non-personal data to improve their predictions — the very promise of big data and algorithmic learning. In doing so, agencies are inviting further sources of algorithmic bias — in some cases overlapping with the prior concerns for proxies — as will be illustrated here.

Suppose in our hypothetical example, the Agency had reason to believe there to be an inverse relationship between the market for a particular product or service and the likelihood that business funds would be used fraudulently — the smaller the market, the higher the likelihood of fraudulent use of funds, and vice versa — and wanted to incorporate market data into the risk model.

---

[176] Privacy Act R.S.C., 1985, c. P-21. Section 6. (emphasis added). Personal information is defined in Section 3 of the *Privacy Act* as "information about an identifiable individual that is recorded in any form." The *Privacy Act* provides examples of personal information including characteristics such as age, marital status and fingerprints; information related to employment history and education; and opinions the individual has expressed directly or attributed to them by another individual. The terms personal data and personal information are used interchangeably in this work.

[177] This is a significant assumption, that could prove difficult to validate practice, however it is one we have chosen to adopt in this work. Challenges to this assumption have been noted by scholars that indicate, for example, that accuracy of personal data is rarely defined in measurable terms, rather that it is assumed to be "obvious." See: Dara Hallinan and Frederik Zuiderveen Borgesius, 'Opinions Can Be Incorrect (in Our Opinion)! On Data Protection Law's Accuracy Principle' (2020) 10 International Data Privacy Law 1 <https://academic.oup.com/idpl/article/10/1/1/5717390>. Further, it is conceivable that data is less accurate for members of groups affected by data ill-suited data collection practices, as described, for example, in: European Commission Directorate-General for Employment Social Affairs and Inclusion, 'Comparative Study on the Collection of Data to Measure the Extent and Impact of Discrimination within the United States, Canada, Australia, the United Kingdom and the Netherlands' (2004) <https://op.europa.eu/en/publication-detail/-/publication/cedfe9eb-9be9-4697-b7be-0551c2523140/language-en> 48–79.

Market data might be licensed or purchased from an external data provider, and combined by the Agency with the personal data to build the risk score. Is the Agency accountable in any way for seeking assurances of accuracy from the data provider regarding the market data, or details as to how is it calculated? Further, consider the possibility that the data provider created the measure of the market as a prediction itself, based on a variety of other input data from other providers, implicating a distributed, multi-actor supply chain in the process. What is the provenance of this data, i.e., the sources and data-collection practices used across the data supply chain, and were they themselves free of errors? Is the calculation of market data a proxy for some other measure?

These are questions that the Agency should be required to investigate for all input data, and the *Privacy Act* makes at least the accuracy question explicit with regard to personal data. Problems with accuracy in the input data, including questions of provenance when such data are procured, are but two examples of known sources of data bias, that in turn implicate algorithmic bias.[178] However, there are currently no legislated requirements for accuracy, provenance or other characteristics of input data *that are not deemed "personal data."* It is intuitively obvious that decision-makers should be held accountable to some standards in these areas for non-personal data, even though specific requirements for accuracy or provenance would be determined by the context at hand. There are federal policies that agencies could draw upon for guidance including the Policy on Service and Digital,[179] and the Government of Canada Digital Standards (Digital Standards),[180] however these are quite general in nature. The Digital Standards Playbook lists, for example, six "aligned behaviours" that intersect with bias and data, although this guidance is high level and does not explicitly address data accuracy or provenance.[181]

Accuracy and provenance of non-personal input data are largely uncovered from a federal governance perspective, based on my review of publicly available sources. This gap is acknowledged somewhat by IRCC in their policy guiding the use of ADM which identifies the need for additional "consultation and oversight" when "non-traditional" data sources are contemplated for use.[182] And the 2018 Data Strategy Roadmap for the Federal Public

---

[178] International Organization for Standardization (n 81) 17 and Section 6.3. See also Karl Werder, Balasubramaniam Ramesh and Rongen (Sophia) Zhang, 'Establishing Data Provenance for Responsible Artificial Intelligence Systems' (2022) 13 ACM Transactions on Management Information Systems 1 <https://dl.acm.org/doi/10.1145/3503488>.

[179] Government of Canada Treasury Board Secretariat, 'Policy on Service and Digital' (n 74).

[180] Government of Canada Treasury Board Secretariat, 'Government of Canada Digital Standards: Playbook' (2021) <https://www.canada.ca/en/government/system/digital-government/government-canada-digital-standards.html>.

[181] Ibid. Section titled Guidance: Design ethical services.

[182] Immigration Refugees and Citizenship Canada (n 87) 7.

Service suggests that governance mechanisms for non-personal data will be considered in the years ahead.[183] In the meantime, ensuring accuracy and provenance of non-personal data must be considered part of making reasonable decisions in the administrative context. Input data that is not accurate, or whose provenance is unknown, could implicate many of the indicia of unreasonableness: lack of a reasonable basis in the evidence, consideration of an irrelevant factor, or lack of a logical connection to the decision. One could argue that the degree to which such input data contributed to algorithmic bias, and the degree to which the resulting algorithmic bias influenced an administrative decision would be mitigating factors especially in the context of proportionality, and this is not in dispute here. However, simply put, making reasonable decisions using non-personal data requires that accuracy and provenance be established in a way that is appropriate to the decision-making context at hand. Until such point that legislated requirements or more specific policy guidelines are put in place, agencies using non-personal input data should establish standards for accuracy and provenance in the use of such data in ML algorithms that provide information to decision-makers.[184]

2.4 STANDARDS FOR THE EVALUATION OF PREDICTIONS

2.4.1 Accuracy of Predictions and Inferences: Uncertainty

When it comes to requirements for accuracy of predictions and inferences made about individuals — i.e., *outputs* of the analysis of personal data, alone or in combination with non-personal data — the situation is no different.

---

[183] Government of Canada, 'Report to the Clerk of the Privy Council: A Data Strategy Roadmap for the Federal Public Service' (2018) <https://www.canada.ca/en/privy-council/corporate/clerk/publications/data-strategy.html>.

[184] Other proposed modernizations of the Privacy Act could be of great help in making reasonable decisions with ML-based ADM. For example, the proposal of "limiting collection" and adopting a "reasonably required" standard could be developed in tandem to a standard for construct validity. A full discussion is outside the scope of this work but we recommend the interested reader see Annex 2 Section 2.2 in the following publication for further information: Government of Canada, 'Modernizing Canada's Privacy Act: Online Public Consultation Discussion Paper' (2020) <https://www.justice.gc.ca/eng/csj-sjc/pa-lprp/dp-dd/raa-rar.html>.

The *Privacy Act* does not mandate accuracy for predictions and inferences. Canada is not alone in this quandary. Wachter and Mittlestadt explored this question in the context of the EU's General Data Protection Regulation (GDPR)[185]. The authors concluded that "Ironically, inferences receive the least protection of all the types of data addressed in data protection law, and yet now pose perhaps the greatest risks in terms of privacy and discrimination."[186] Justice Canada is considering this issue for future modernizations of the *Privacy Act*, stating that it may:

> ... specify that personal information that a federal public body **creates or derives by making inferences** based on an individual's personal information, or information about other individuals, would qualify as a collection of personal information.[187]

Applied to the hypothetical scenario, the risk-score prediction provokes an inference about an applicant's proclivity for fraudulent use of funds. The inference being made is a personal characteristic that describes an individual. If the *Privacy Act* were, in the future, updated to consider inferences a "collection" of personal information, then the *Privacy Act*'s accuracy requirements would apply to inferences as well. However, even if the *Privacy Act* were so amended, the problem would remain that there is no single trusted measure of "accuracy" for predictions in ML, a problem which cascades to inferences drawn from those predictions as well. We will briefly highlight some of the challenges with the concept and measurement of accuracy in an ML setting.

In ML terminology, the word "accuracy" typically refers narrowly to predictive accuracy. In a simple classification exercise, predictive accuracy is commonly assessed by comparing the ML model's performance against a holdout sample, for which the answers are known. Or, if the ML is making a prediction of an output along a continuous scale, accuracy could be assessed by looking at how well the model accounts for variability in the outputs. There are different ways to calculate predictive accuracy based on the nature of the ML model itself and its predictive task, but in general, predictive accuracy measures are focused on how the model performs its predictive tasks

---

[185] REGULATION (EU) 2016/679 OF THE EUROPEAN PARLIAMENT AND OF THE COUNCIL (General Data Protection Regulation) 2016. < https://gdpr-info.eu/>

[186] Sandra Wachter and Brent Mittelstadt, 'A Right to Reasonable Inferences: Re-Thinking Data Protection Law in the Age of Big Data and AI' (2019) 2019 Columbia business law review 494, 575.

[187] Government of Canada, 'Modernizing Canada's Privacy Act: Online Public Consultation Discussion Paper' (n 184) 13 (emphasis added).

within the scope and values of the data it has been presented with. Predictive accuracy metrics don't account for any of the concepts described earlier with respect to standards – i.e., validity, representativeness of data, and proxy variables. Therefore, predictive accuracy metrics can be high even when there are underlying problems with the model or the data that lead to algorithmic bias. This is a major challenge in ML, that decision-makers inherit, and who scholars have cautioned against being "simultaneously rational and unfair" by relying on accurate yet invalid inferences.[188]

Against this backdrop, Wachter and Mittlestadt proposed a novel approach to the problem of accuracy of inferences: a multi-faceted disclosure which would effectively substantiate the inference, taking into account both the data and the model. The three requirements of this disclosure are:

1. why certain data form a normatively acceptable basis from which to draw inferences;
2. why these inferences are relevant and normatively acceptable for the chosen processing purpose or type of automated decision; and
3. whether the data and methods used to draw the inferences are accurate and statistically reliable.[189]

Although their disclosure was proposed in the context of fully automated algorithmic decision-making for gaps in EU data privacy and protection law, its elements can be applied here to the use of ML to provide information to assist an administrative decision-maker in the Canadian context.

Imagine judicial review of an administrative decision where the inference used to inform the decision-maker could not satisfy the elements of Wachter and Mittlestadt's disclosure. It is hard to see how such a decision would be seen by a court as reasonable at all. For example, how would the factors used to construct the inference be seen as relevant without satisfying element (1); how would the inference be shown to provide evidence for the decision without satisfying element number (2); and, how would the inference be deemed to contribute to consistency in decision-making without satisfying element (3)? Wachter and Mittlestadt's proposed disclosure supports the need for a standard for inferences, and reinforces the standards we have already proposed. The first two elements of the proposed disclosure encompass the elements of construct validity and knowledge limits. The third element connects to standards for measurement validity and the avoidance of proxies on

---

[188] Frederick F Schauer, Profiles, Probabilities, and Stereotypes (Harvard University Press 2006), as cited in Barocas and Selbst (n 171) 688.

[189] Wachter and Mittelstadt (n 186) 501.

input and output variables, and it includes the need for accuracy and provenance on input data.

With respect to the concept of statistical reliability mentioned in the third element, Wachter and Mittlestadt offer little by way of explanation of this requirement, except that it might be achieved "via statistical verification techniques."[190] In general, the concept of statistical reliability is understood to have its roots in the social science domain of psychometrics and it describes the consistency of a measurement process[191] i.e., given the same inputs, a statistically reliable measurement process will produce the same result. We describe an operational approach that addresses the concept of reliability in the administrative context in Section 2.4.2, namely Kroll and others' proposal for procedural regularity.

The mention of "methods" as part of the Wachter and Mittlestadt's proposed disclosure is also unclear, and they do not elaborate on this in the original article. Only a reference to section 28 (b) in Germany's 2010 data protection law is provided as background and which states that: "The methods being used are sound according to the state of the art in science, mathematics, or statistics ..."[192] There are at least two problems with recommending the use of methods that are sound and state of the art. First, the universe of ML methods is vast and constantly evolving, and the characterization of a method as sound or state of the art is entirely context dependent — one method may be perfectly sound for one application context and completely inappropriate for another — methods are not universally sound.[193] Second, even if a method were deemed sound in a particular context and further met an appropriate threshold of predictive accuracy — this doesn't mean that an accurate inference will result. As discussed, sound methods can produce results high in predictive accuracy, but their inferences can still be biased. What is needed to more completely substantiate the accuracy of inferences, is a broader and more

---

[190] Ibid. 585.

[191] Paul C Price, Rajiv Jhangiani and I-Chant A. Chian, 'Reliability and Validity of Measurement' (*Research Methods in Psychology — 2nd Canadian Edition*, 2020) <https://opentextbc.ca/researchmethods/chapter/reliability-and-validity-of-measurement/>.

[192] Wachter and Mittlestadt (n 186) 587.

[193] This is also the reason why we have deliberately not proposed standards anywhere in this work related to the choice of specific algorithms, which would need to be tailored to the specific policy and decision-making context. Note however that federal guidance is provided in the choice of algorithm for agencies using ADM (see: Government of Canada, 'Guideline on Service and Digital' (2023) <https://www.canada.ca/en/government/system/digital-government/guideline-service-digital.html#ToC4> Section 4.5.3). Tutt also provides a provocative approach to classifying algorithms within the standards setting work of an administrative agency (see: Andrew Tutt, 'AN FDA FOR ALGORITHMS' (2017) 69 Administrative law review 83, 107–109).

explicit basis for evaluation of the *predictions* (rather than the *methods*). While predictive accuracy — appropriate to the algorithmic and policy context at hand — is important and should remain part of the evaluation, we propose that measures of uncertainty must be used in complement, as we explain now. The word "accurate" connotes a falsely binary conception, that an inference is either accurate or it's not. In ML, uncertainty is a given: ML predictions from which inferences are drawn will always have some level of uncertainty associated with them.[194] It follows that in a culture of justification characterized by rationality and fairness, agencies must explicitly consider the sources of uncertainty in their use of ADM and act accordingly. Those impacted by an ADM could reasonably ask how certain the decision-maker was about the predictions and inferences that helped inform their decision, and decision-makers that do not know the answer are flying blind without any basis for justification.

Uncertainty measures have not historically or consistently been used to qualify ML results for a variety of reasons such as the prevalence of other measures of evaluation,[195] or because they have been difficult to derive for more complex ML algorithms. Nonetheless, uncertainty is now gaining focus in ML research. For example, Hüllermeier and Waegeman describe two types of uncertainty in ML.[196] Aleatoric uncertainty describes uncertainty associated with the statistical characteristics of the ML model, and overlaps with the concept of predictive accuracy we have discussed here. This concept of uncertainty also incorporates the familiar concept of confidence intervals associated with a particular prediction in the use of linear regression. Epistemic uncertainty describes uncertainty associated with whether or not the right model has been designed, and overlaps with the concepts of construct validity and measurement validity we have discussed here.

Aleatoric and epistemic uncertainty have been recognized as a source of algorithmic bias by NIST, who counsel ML developers to continuously monitor and address the potential impacts of such uncertainty.[197] Accordingly, agencies using ADM must examine the uncertainty inherent in the ML algorithms they are using, for their bias-inducing effects on the predictions and inferences informing decision-makers. Agencies must determine how

---

[194] This is true because ML (as defined in this work) is probabilistic, not deterministic.

[195] Christian (n 171). See Chapter 9 titled 'Uncertainty'.

[196] Eyke Hüllermeier and Willem Waegeman, 'Aleatoric and Epistemic Uncertainty in Machine Learning: An Introduction to Concepts and Methods' (2021) 110 Machine Learning 457, 458.

[197] Schwartz and others (n 66) 20–21 and 27–28. Note that NIST highlights uncertainty particularly for large scale AI models such as large language models, whose biased predictions have been exposed extensively in the ML literature. However, considerations of uncertainty are applicable to any ML model scenario.

much uncertainty can be tolerated in any specific decision-making context. Technical methods for measuring and managing uncertainty in ML remain immature, however even now agencies should consider the potential bias-inducing effects of both aleatoric and epistemic uncertainty, and implement standards accordingly, at the very least in qualitative terms.

2.4.2 Individual Fairness

ML models do not describe one individual; they describe patterns in aggregate across many. Minimizing algorithmic bias helps to mitigate disparate impact in the outcomes of the algorithm, *as a whole*. However when an algorithm is deemed to be fair and unbiased as a whole, the same cannot be said for every individual subject to the model's predictions — predictions at the individual level may still exhibit the effects of algorithmic bias.[198] This has been described as "a serious methodological challenge to the use of machine learning."[199] Further, even when an algorithm processes data from one very well-defined group, and generates predictions only for members of that group, the degree to which bias is exhibited will vary across the individuals to which it is applied. Sociotechnical scholars have described the "homogenizing effect" of algorithms that are a poor fit for people who are more the exception than the rule, or those whose distinguishing characteristics were never considered by the model in the first place.[200] In short, an individual could reasonably ask: just because the algorithm is well-behaved overall, are the predictions it makes fair and unbiased for *me*?

This simple question strikes at the heart of the application of ADM systems in the administrative context: how to resolve the "fundamental tension" in the orientation of ADM systems — developed based on patterns across many — with the need to justify administrative decisions at the level of the individual.[201] If decisions cannot be justified for the individual, the decision could be taken to have considered an irrelevant factor, i.e., a group-level prediction that is not relevant for the individual. Additionally, lack of justification at an individual

---

[198] Coglianese and Lehr (n 118) 36. See also the NIST discussion of the "ecological fallacy," wherein models developed for a specified group exhibit biased results for *individual* members of the group: Schwartz and others (n 66) 23. See also Coglianese (n 123) 58.

[199] David Danks, 'Learning' in Keith Frankish and William M Ramsey (eds), *The Cambridge Handbook of Artificial Intelligence* (Cambridge University Press 2014) 158.

[200] Ali Alkhatib, 'To Live in Their Utopia: Why Algorithmic Systems Create Absurd Outcomes', *CHI Conference on Human Factors in Computing Systems (CHI '21), May 8–13, 2021, Yokohama, Japan.* (ACM 2021) 9.

[201] Hermstrüwer (n 174) 202.

level is related to unexplained inconsistency in decision-making — as will be described in further detail shortly. The challenges posed by the need for individual-level justifications have also been noted in the domain of international human rights law, that shares an orientation to the rights and interests of the individuals with administrative law. Scholars from both domains have described implications of this contradiction from each of their perspectives.

For example, Alston commented that using predictions made from historical, group-level data to infer individual-level behaviour shifts the responsibility for entrenched structural factors from institutions to individuals.[202] McGregor explained that because rights cannot be interfered with arbitrarily under international human rights law, "where an individual's rights are interfered with by a decision involving algorithms, the underlying reasoning must be made on the basis of factors specific and relevant to that individual."[203] Group-based models that predict future behaviour neglect important factors such as individual agency and choice,[204] implicating what Citron and Pasquale cite as "arbitrariness by algorithm."[205] Cobbe explains that "it is often impossible to predict the behaviour of any one individual from knowledge of the collective behaviour of a group to which they belong. ... This is a problem for ADM systems, which risk turning group-level differences into discriminatory decisions which affect individuals."[206] Further, a decision-maker that relies only on group inferences to make a decision impacting an individual could be seen as fettering their decision contrary to procedural fairness if specific facts relevant to the individual are not appropriately considered.[207]

Some authors have suggested that administrative law principles should be revisited in light of this tension,[208] which is an important question however not one that we undertake within the scope of this work. There has been some

---

[202] Philip Alston, 'Report of the Special Rapporteur on Extreme Poverty and Human Rights A/74/493' (2019) <https://undocs.org/A/74/493> 11.

[203] Lorna McGregor, Daragh Murray and Vivian Ng, 'INTERNATIONAL HUMAN RIGHTS LAW AS A FRAMEWORK FOR ALGORITHMIC ACCOUNTABILITY' (2019) 68 International and Comparative Law Quarterly 309, 337.

[204] Ibid.

[205] The term "arbitrariness by algorithm" was coined by US Federal Trade Commission Chairwoman Edith Ramirez in 2013, as cited in: Danielle Keats Citron and Frank A Pasquale, 'The Scored Society: Due Process for Automated Predictions' (2014) 89(1) Washington law review, 24.

[206] Cobbe (n 98) 653.

[207] Ibid. 646. See also Daly (n 88) 16–18. Note that the issue of fettering applies more to fully automated decision-making than where an ADM systems is providing information only to assist the decision-maker.

[208] Jennifer Raso and Teresa Scassa, 'Administrative Law and the Governance of Automated Decision-Making' (25 September 2020) https://www.youtube.com/watch?v=nVs46EMAHRo accessed 28 November 2020. See also Scassa (n 60). See also: Raso (n 6) 182.

research into methods to technically codify a requirement for individual-level fairness into ML algorithms, however many of these are beset by stringent assumptions and practical limitations to their deployment.[209] While there are no easy solutions, agencies must still take this question seriously: Are ML predictions that are used to inform decision-makers fair at the individual level? *How* seriously to take this question and *how* fair to individual the predictions should be is a matter of procedural fairness. Recall Section 2.1.3 and the guidance from *Baker*: "The duty of procedural fairness is flexible and variable and depends on an appreciation of the context of the particular statute and the rights affected."[210] So the answer to these questions of procedural fairness depends upon the context. However, what is certain is that agencies cannot neglect to consider it.[211] With respect to the substantive aspects of individual fairness, i.e., how ML predictions derived from group results are evaluated for individual-level bias, research is sparse, however we describe three (somewhat overlapping) approaches proposed in the literature.

One recommendation is that explanations be developed that articulate, for each individual, which of their characteristics — captured as inputs or features in the algorithm — was determinative of the algorithm's prediction and the decision-maker's subsequent inference.[212] Here, the explanation is taken to satisfy the need for individual fairness. It is a given that the algorithm must be both explainable and interpretable for this solution to be feasible, which in itself is a difficult pre-requisite to make in ML, although the "reviewability" framework proposed by Cobbe, Lee, and Singh (see discussion in Section 2.1.2) provides a starting point.[213]

The second is similar to the first but centres more on counterfactual reasoning. Hermstrüwer suggests that using ML in the administrative context requires "some description of the things that the person concerned would have to change in order to obtain a different decision"[214] and proposes that agencies examine counterfactual scenarios as part of the initial testing of the system.[215]

[209] Alexandra Chouldechova and Aaron Roth, 'A Snapshot of the Frontiers of Fairness in Machine Learning' (2020) 63(5) Communications of the ACM, 85.

[210] *Baker v. Minister of Citizenship and Immigration* (n 39) 819.

[211] Daly also proposed a useful model within which to examine the interaction between rationality and fairness in the administrative context, that is recommended for all readers. See Daly (n 88) 13–15.

[212] Coglianese and Lehr (n 118). 34–36. See also: Andrew Selbst and Solon Barocas, 'THE INTUITIVE APPEAL OF EXPLAINABLE MACHINES' (2018) 87 Fordham law review 1085; Finale Doshi-Velez and Been Kim, 'Towards A Rigorous Science of Interpretable Machine Learning' (2017) <https://arxiv.org/abs/1702.08608> both as cited in Hermstrüwer (n 174) 212.

[213] Cobbe, Lee, and Singh (n 126).

[214] Hermstrüwer (n 174) 204.

[215] Ibid. 212.

The third is directly linked to one of the indicia of unreasonableness, i.e., unexplained inconsistency in administrative decisions. The premise is this: If the algorithm is producing different predictions for individuals who are deemed "like," and doing so for reasons unknown, then this could be seen as giving rise to unreasonable decisions due to inconsistency. The difficulty here is in mathematically defining what "like" individuals means in measurable terms captured by the input data — a complex question that intersects with emerging ML research on fairness metrics.[216] Nevertheless, the evaluation of an algorithmic system for consistency in the results it produces is clearly important.

To this end, Kroll and others propose an operational requirement to prove "procedural regularity" in algorithmic systems, which certifies that the procedures used to design and develop the algorithm apply to all individuals equally, and in no way disadvantage any particular individual.[217] Key features of this requirement include that:

- The decision policy was fully specified (and this choice of policy was recorded reliably) before the particular decision subjects were known, reducing the ability to design the process to disadvantage a particular individual.
- Each decision is reproducible from the specified decision policy and the inputs for that decision.[218]

Kroll and others illustrate how emerging mathematical and computational techniques can be used to achieve procedural regularity. Even as these techniques mature and become more widely understood and available, agencies should consider the procedural regularity requirements proposed by Kroll and others and examine how to approach these requirements within the methods currently available to them.

Individual fairness is integral to the objectives of administrative decision-making. Scholars across legal and ML domains acknowledge the

---

[216] See, e.g., Kroll and others (n 86) 687–690. See also Sorelle A Friedler and others, 'A Comparative Study of Fairness-Enhancing Interventions in Machine Learning', *Proceedings of the Conference on Fairness, Accountability, and Transparency* (ACM 2019) <https://dl.acm.org/doi/10.1145/3287560.3287589>; Sam Corbett-Davies and Sharad Goel (n 172); International Organization for Standardization (n 83) 14–27; Alice Xiang, 'Reconciling Legal and Technical Approaches to Algorithmic Bias' (2021) 88 Tennessee Law Review 649 705–723.

[217] Kroll and others (n 86) 656. While this proposal for procedural regularity was made in the context of fully automated decisions systems, it remains a useful model for ADM that is used to assist the decision-maker.

[218] Ibid. 657.

difficulties that predictions based on group characteristics pose to fulfilling guarantees of individual fairness. Three conceptual approaches to individual fairness have been presented here, and while their mathematical implementations remain under development, it is imperative that agencies make efforts to evaluate how questions of individual fairness manifest in their use of ADM, and put in place standards relating to individual fairness even if qualitative in nature. Without such standards, agencies would surely be challenged to justify decisions that impact individuals, and would risk implicating indicia of unreasonableness including use of an irrelevant factor and unexplained inconsistency in decision-making.

2.5 CHAPTER SUMMARY: PROPOSED STANDARDS FOR THE CONTROL OF ALGORITHMIC BIAS

In this chapter, we have proposed a series of standards for the control of algorithmic bias derived from the principles of administrative law. Table 2.1 lists these standards, categorized according to those focused on mitigating the creation of biased predictions and inferences, and those used to evaluate predictions and inferences. All of the proposed standards in Table 2.1 are for

TABLE 2.1   Proposed standards for the control of algorithmic bias

STANDARDS TO MITIGATE THE CREATION OF BIASED PREDICTIONS

Overall:
  1. Construct validity
  2. Knowledge limits

Model input data (spanning personal and non-personal information):
  3. Accuracy and provenance
  4. Measurement validity
  5. Representativeness

Model target of prediction:
  6. Measurement validity
  7. Match to policy objective

STANDARDS FOR THE EVALUATION OF PREDICTIONS
8. Uncertainty   9. Individual fairness

use in the design and development of ML algorithms, before the ADM system is implemented.

Standards 1 through 7 each address one specific source of algorithmic bias — we refer to these as *individual* standards. In contrast, standards 8 and 9 address overall qualities of the model and the predictions that are shaped by the degree to which the individual standards were effective in the *aggregate*. Because our work is illustrative and not exhaustive, there are undoubtedly additional sources of bias for which individual standards could be proposed, and which would impact the evaluations inherent in the aggregate standards. Both individual and aggregate standards are needed.

All of the standards presented in Table 2.1, along with the additional standards for the measure of disparity in outcomes that we present in the following chapter, are stated generically without reference to a particular policy context or ADM use case. Agencies would need to further specify these standards according to the circumstances at hand. And, they would need to do so in a proportional manner, ensuring the standards are implemented in way that is appropriate to the level of impact of the decision. These and other implementation considerations for the full set of proposed standards are discussed in Chapter 4.

Substantive Equality and Standards for the Measurement of Disparity

3

In the previous chapter, we proposed procedural standards for the control of algorithmic bias based on reasonableness review in administrative law. Say an agency has adopted all of these standards — how will the agency know if these standards have actually proven effective in achieving the intended purpose of mitigating disparate impact in the outcomes of administrative decisions? The only way to definitively know this is to examine the actual decisions and outcomes that result from the ADM when it is fully operational. Agencies should put in place monitoring schemes to do so over time, and inspect whether there is evidence of disparate impact in the outcomes on an ongoing basis. However, our interest here is in the use of standards *in advance of deployment* — to anticipate and prevent disparate impact. Agencies that do so have insight into the potential outcomes of their decisions, enabling them to: strengthen the basis of justification for their use of ADM to achieve their intended policy objectives; avoid the creation of undue hardship for impacted individuals; and, be confident that their use of ADM is aligned with the *Charter* guarantee of substantive equality.

Before proceeding, we must emphasize the difference between predictions, decisions and outcomes. For example, in the illustrative scenario we have been using, suppose an applicant's *predicted* risk score was high which caused the Agency to deny them any funding. The *decision* is the denial of

DOI: 10.1201/b23364-3

funding and the *outcome* is how this decision plays out for this applicant in their life. Anticipating how a *prediction* will influence a *decision* and what *outcome* that will create for an individual is compounding hypotheticals, especially given our focus on predictions that are used to inform a decision-maker but are not fully determinative of a decision. However, we argue that examination of *disparity of the predictions* — which we define as the degree to which the predictions differ according to group classifications that are grounds for discrimination under the *Charter* — is a good place to start in terms of standards. Further, we argue that an agency using ADM must establish a testing strategy to examine disparity in predictions, according to the standards we propose, before implementing the ADM system.

How much, precisely, must the measured outcome between groups differ such that it constitutes discrimination? The nature and weight of statistical methods used to support a reviewing court's inquiry, the role of legislative intent, and the relevance of whether the impugned state action caused the alleged disparate impact in question have been evolving in jurisprudence.[219] Scholars and government bodies have struggled to establish consensus on what specific measures and thresholds for disparity should consist of and have debated the role of statistical tests of significance in assessing disparity. Even after decades of study and court interpretations, there are no precise answers to what constitutes disparity.[220] In some ways, this is unsurprising because what will be interpreted as disparity will vary based on the context within which it is being assessed. A measured level of disparity that is considered unacceptable in one circumstance may be trivial in another. Nonetheless, understanding some of the history of how disparity is measured is important background for this work. In keeping with the premise of this work that standards should first be derived from legal principles and existing norms, our focus will be to uncover how disparity is measured and interpreted in policy and legal sources, and apply these insights to developing generally applicable procedural standards for measuring disparity in predictions.

This chapter will proceed as follows. First, we examine the measure of disparity in the *prima facie test* of discrimination for section 15 *Charter* challenges. These findings will then be synthesized with the SCC's recent

---

[219] For the evolution prior to *Fraser v. Canada (Attorney General)* [2020] SCC 28, see, e.g., Evelyn Braun, 'Adverse Effect Discrimination: Proving the *Prima Facie* Case' (2005) 11 Review of constitutional studies 119. See also Béatrice Vizkelety, *Proving Discrimination in Canada* (Carswell 1987) 133–192; Sheppard (n 11) 37–64.

[220] *Fraser v. Canada (Attorney General)* [2020] SCC 28. (hereinafter "*Fraser*") at para 59. See also detailed discussion and case examples provided in Vizkelety (n 217) at 178 fn 181 and 179 fn 182. For a comparative discussion of the European context, see: Sandra Fredman, *Discrimination Law* (2nd ed., Oxford University Press 2011) 153–231.

interpretations of the measure of disparity in their decision in *Fraser v. Canada (Attorney General)*,[221] in order to propose a modern set of standards for the measure of disparity, including the use of disaggregated data which is central to the measurement of disparity itself. This chapter concludes with five proposed standards for the measurement of disparity.

3.1 THE MEASURE OF DISPARITY IN THE *PRIMA FACIE* TEST OF DISCRIMINATION

The level of disparity between groups on any particular measured outcome is the central question to be answered in determining whether there has been a *prima facie* violation of equality guarantees. Challenges to the *Charter's* substantive equality guarantee require courts to determine whether the impugned law, policy, action, or administrative decision has a discriminatory effect on the party raising the challenge. In doing so, courts assess the context and extent of the alleged disparate impact (also known as adverse effects) to determine if violations of substantive equality have occurred.[222]

In order to determine if there has been a *prima facie* violation of the equality guarantee, the court first asks whether "the impugned law or state action":

1. on its face or in its impact, creates a distinction based on an enumerated or analogous ground; and,
2. imposes burdens or denies a benefit in a manner that has the effect of reinforcing, perpetuating, or exacerbating disadvantage. [223]

The second step of a court's inquiry, if a *prima facie* case of discrimination has been established, is to determine whether the rights infringed upon are justified either as an ameliorative measure under section 15(2) of the *Charter* or justified as a reasonable limit according to section 1 of the *Charter*. The second step is a contextually sensitive inquiry into the

---

[221] *Fraser v. Canada (Attorney General)* (n 220).

[222] Sheppard (n 11) 19–23. See also: Robert J Sharpe and Kent Roach, *The Charter of Rights and Freedoms* (6th edn, Irwin Law Inc 2017) 354–406.

[223] *Fraser v. Canada (Attorney General)* (n 220) para 27. The two steps of the test have evolved in their precise requirements through decisions in several cases, as elaborated in Jonnette Watson Hamilton, 'Cautious Optimism: Fraser v Canada (Attorney General)' (2021) 30 Constitutional Forum / Forum constitutionnel 1. at pp. 3–10.

justification for the limitation of a right, whose examination is outside the scope of this work.

Examining the basis for a *prima facie* violation is a comparative exercise,[224] in which the effects of the state action on the party alleging disparate impact are evaluated against the effects on a benchmark comparator group.[225] The feature(s) that define the alleging party as a group may be a direct reflection of one of the enumerated or analogous grounds of discrimination (e.g., the party is a woman who alleges the ground of sex), or indirectly linked to grounds of discrimination (e.g., part-time workers, who as a group are comprised mostly of women).[226] In either case, the court first examines whether or not there is evidence of disparate impact, by comparing the characteristics and experiences of the party alleging discrimination with that of the chosen comparator group to determine whether the effects of the law are different for the two groups. How *disparity* is measured is central to this inquiry.

3.2 LEGISLATIVE AND POLICY APPROACHES TO THE MEASUREMENT OF DISPARITY

In this section, we draw from the domain of employment equity in both the United States and Canada, within which much of the policy and precedent pertaining to the measurement of disparity has been situated. One of the concrete examples of a measure of disparity (which is referred to in the quote that follows as "adverse impact" and is equivalent for present purposes) is the "four-fifths" rule put in place by the US Equal Employment Opportunity Commission, which states that:

> A selection rate for any race, sex, or ethnic group which is less than four-fifths (4/5) (or eighty percent) of the rate for the group with the highest rate

---

[224] Sheppard (n 11) 44–46.

[225] Scholars have noted that the choice of the comparator groups is highly determinative of the outcome of the *prima facie* inquiry. A full discussion of this analysis is outside the scope of this work, however for additional reading, see, e.g., the discussion in Sheppard (n11). 44–46. See also Jennifer Koshan and Jonnette Watson Hamilton, 'Tugging at the Strands: Adverse Effects Discrimination and the Supreme Court Decision in Fraser' (2020) <https://ablawg.ca/2020/11/09/tugging-at-the-strands-adverse-effects-discrimination-and-the-supreme-court-decision-in-fraser/> 8–10.

[226] Braun (n 219) 125–127.

will generally be regarded by the Federal enforcement agencies as evidence of adverse impact, while a greater than four-fifths rate will generally not be regarded by Federal enforcement agencies as evidence of adverse impact.[227]

This rule is used in a forward-looking manner to create guidelines and to inform monitoring to protect against adverse effects,[228] and it has been cited extensively since 1978 when it began to be used in US court cases alleging disparate impact.[229] In practice, this rule is less rigid than its introductory text quoted above implies, and it provides additional guidance that addresses the impact of small and large sample sizes in detecting differences between selection rates, and measures of statistical significance of differences between selection rates. While simple to understand and implement, the four-fifths rule suffers from several methodological weaknesses, and has been both lauded and criticized by United States, Canadian, and international scholars.[230] In her in-depth study of measures of adverse effects in Canada, the United States, and Europe, Braun concludes that the four-fifths rule is now used by courts simply as a "starting point" in their examination of a *prima facie* case of adverse effects discrimination, rather than a measure that is sufficient on its own.[231]

In Canada, the *Employment Equity Act* sets out obligations for the federal government and the federally regulated private sector in order to advance substantive equality in these workplaces.[232] Legally mandated data collection, monitoring, and reporting practices assist these employers in assessing the characteristics of the labour market, and determining whether the proportion of actual employees, classified according to sex, Aboriginal and visible minority status meets targets set at the national or industry sectoral level (known as the "attainment rate").[233] While attainment rate and qualitative

---

[227] Equal Employment Opportunity Commission Information on Impact 1978 29 CFR § 1607.4.

[228] European Commission Directorate-General for Employment Social Affairs and Inclusion (n 177) 40–41.

[229] Braun (n 219) 129–131.

[230] See, e.g., Kingsley R Browne, 'Statistical Proof of Discrimination: Beyond "Damned Lies"' (1994) 15 Berkeley journal of employment and labor law 176; Vizkelety (n 219). Chapter 4; Braun (n 219). 129–131; Barocas and Selbst (n 171) 701–702; European Commission Directorate-General for Employment Social Affairs and Inclusion (n 177) 40–41.

[231] Braun (n 219) 130.

[232] Employment Equity Act S.C. 1995, c. 44.

[233] Government of Canada, 'Employment Equity Act: Annual Report 2020' (2020) <https://www.canada.ca/en/employment-social-development/corporate/portfolio/labour/programs/employment-equity/reports/2020-annual.html>. See also Government of Canada Treasury Board Secretariat, 'Employment Equity in the Public Service of Canada for Fiscal Year 2019 to 2020' <https://www.canada.ca/en/government/publicservice/wellness-inclusion-diversity-public-service/diversity-inclusion-public-service/employment-equity-annual-reports/employment-equity-public-service-canada-2019-2020.html>.

evaluations of disparity are provided in the reports, there are no hard and fast measures of what constitutes "too much" disparity.

The Government of Ontario has published *Anti-Racism Data Standards* policy which provides guidance to public-sector organizations (PSOs) on how to calculate racial disproportionality and disparity indices.[234] However, it stops short of providing specific thresholds, such as the 80% figure stated in the US four-fifths rule, against which to evaluate such indices, instead offering the following guidance:

> Appropriate and meaningful thresholds are expected to vary based on the nature and context of the outcome being assessed …. PSOs are encouraged to establish an advisory committee to support the analysis and interpretation of findings. To provide a diversity of perspectives, advisory committees could include clients, members of affected committees, subject matter experts, and internal and external stakeholders and partners.[235]

These legislative and policy mechanisms illustrate several important themes in the measurement of disparity. First, each of them is oriented to group comparisons across a small number of very specific characteristics such as race, sex, ethnicity, Aboriginal or visible minority status. Second, over time scholars and policy makers have adopted a more context-sensitive and less rigid approach to what constitutes disparity. And third, *all* of these mechanisms rely on the collection of disaggregated data for implementation. The collection and use of disaggregated data presents many unique challenges, which we elaborate on following the analysis of *Fraser*. *Fraser*, to which we now turn, illustrates the SCC's comprehensive approach to assessing disparity, expanding upon the first two aforementioned themes.

3.3 THE SUPREME COURT OF CANADA ON MEASURES OF DISPARITY IN *FRASER*

In *Fraser*, the SCC examined the Royal Canadian Mounted Police (RCMP) job-sharing program against the claim that it was discriminatory against women. In the program, full-time employees were permitted to temporarily change their status to part-time workers, however in doing so their part-time

---

[234] Government of Ontario, 'Data Standards for the Identification and Monitoring of Systemic Racism' (2020) <https://www.ontario.ca/document/data-standards-identification-and-monitoring-systemic-racism>.

[235] Ibid. Standard 32

earnings were no longer treated as pensionable earnings. While the program's stipulations regarding pensionable earnings applied equally to all program participants regardless of their sex, it differed from other RCMP programs that continued pension credit during other periods of work interruption such as suspension or unpaid leave. The claimants argued that the job-sharing program had an adverse effect on women in violation of the *Charter* equality guarantee. The majority decision indeed found the job-sharing program to be discriminatory against women, the only adverse effects case recorded in Canada thus far to succeed in proving discrimination on the basis of sex.[236] Writing for the majority, Justice Abella summarized the reasons for the decision as follows:

> The relevant evidence showed that RCMP members who worked reduced hours in the job-sharing program were predominantly women with young children. These statistics were bolstered by compelling evidence about the disadvantages women face as a group in balancing professional and domestic work. This evidence shows the clear association between gender and fewer or less stable working hours, and demonstrates that the RCMP's use of a temporary reduction in working hours as a basis for imposing less favourable pension consequences has an adverse impact on women.[237]

Several observations can be drawn from this decision to inform forward-looking standards for the measurement of disparity.

First, the majority in *Fraser* reinforced that in examining the claim of discrimination, the Court must arrive at a broad contextual understanding of "the actual situation of the group and the potential of the impugned law to worsen their [circumstances]."[238] Citing scholar Colleen Sheppard, whose work elaborates the contribution of process-based systemic contributors to disparate impact,[239] Justice Abella highlighted the importance of considering ongoing institutional practices for their contribution to disparate impact.[240] In *Fraser*, what this meant was that the Court considered the impacts of the job-sharing policies in the context of the broader challenges experienced by working women caring for young children. The Court's assessment of the impacts of the job-sharing policies was not one-dimensional, it was not limited to the measured impacts within the work environment. Instead, it considered whether the impacts of the policies were contrary to guarantees of substantive equality, taking into account a broader societal context.

---

[236] Hamilton (n 223) 1.
[237] *Fraser v. Canada (Attorney General)* (n 220) 11.
[238] Ibid at para 173, citing Withler v. Canada (Attorney General) [2011] 1 SCR 396 at para 37.
[239] Sheppard (n 11).
[240] *Fraser v. Canada (Attorney General)* (n 220) at para 31 and 35.

Second, the majority rejected a strict "mirror comparator" analysis as necessary to the process of determining whether there was a *prima facie* violation of the *Charter* equality guarantee.[241] A mirror comparator analysis is one in which the claimants must be compared to a group that is "like the claimants in all ways save for the characteristics relating to the alleged ground of discrimination."[242] Although considered formalistic by many scholars, the mirror comparator analysis had been deemed necessary by courts prior to *Fraser*.[243] It had proved difficult to achieve in practice, resulting in adverse effects cases lost due to the deficiencies in the method of comparison itself — for example, the inability to identify an appropriate comparator group.[244] The majority in *Fraser* instead cited multiple comparisons as evidence[245] and relied upon computationally simple statistics that were nonetheless power-fully demonstrative of disparate impact.[246]

Third, the SCC made very clear that the effect of the law is what matters in discerning a *prima facie* case of adverse effects discrimination. The legisla-tive intent behind the law, the claimant's choices (e.g., a claimant's choice to participate in the RCMP's job-sharing program), and whether the impugned state action caused the alleged adverse effects were all disregarded by the majority in the assessment of adverse effects discrimination.[247] The majority also elaborated that the effects of the law need not be uniform across all mem-bers of the group thought to be adversely affected (i.e., women, in *Fraser*).[248]

Fourth, the statistical evidence presented in *Fraser,* that the majority of the employees in the job-sharing program were women with young chil-dren, clearly showed a pattern that persisted over time.[249] Commentators have noted that the strength of the evidence was an important, unique feature in *Fraser* that may not be present in other cases.[250] Despite the clarity of the evidence in *Fraser*, Justice Abella elaborated on the purpose and challenges of statistical evidence in substantive equality cases in her decision,[251] drawing

---

[241] Ibid. at para 94.

[242] *Auton (Guardian ad litem of) v. British Columbia (Attorney General)* [2004] SCC 78 at para 55.

[243] Sheppard (n 11). 44–46.

[244] Ibid.

[245] Hamilton (n 223) 7.

[246] *Fraser v. Canada (Attorney General)* (n 220). at para 97.

[247] Ibid. at para 69–71.

[248] Ibid. at para 72. Conceptually, this is well aligned with the conclusion that what is fair for the group may not be fair for the individual — the challenge of individual fairness in the use of ADM in the administrative context as described in Section 2.4.2.

[249] Ibid. at para 97.

[250] Commentary from lawyer Heather Hettiarachchi as cited in Dale Smith, 'An Equitable Outcome' [2020] *CBA National* <https://nationalmagazine.ca/en-ca/articles/law/in-depth/2020/an-equitable-outcome>.

[251] *Fraser v. Canada (Attorney General)* (n 220) at para 57–67.

heavily from scholars and case law in Canada and internationally, noting that quantitative data may not be available for the groups of interest,[252] nor be of sufficient quality for fine-grained statistical comparisons. Justice Abella underscored the importance that courts look at the interplay between qualitative and quantitative information, in order "to establish a disparate pattern of exclusion or harm that is statistically significant and not simply the results of chance" for the *prima facie* case of adverse effects discrimination.[253] In other words, measures of statistical significance should not be read in isolation, but rather considered in light of qualitative information to create a coherent understanding of what the observed patterns mean.

What *Fraser* did not directly address was intersectionality: "the unique forms of discrimination, oppression and marginalization that can result from the interplay of two or more identity-based grounds of discrimination."[254] Prior to *Fraser*, the SCC had never considered intersectionality in *Charter* cases.[255] While Justice Abella clearly acknowledged the "uneven division of childcare responsibilities" that disadvantages women in Canadian society,[256] she deemed it unnecessary to pursue an intersectional analysis in *Fraser* because discrimination on the basis of sex had been so clearly proven.[257] Nonetheless, in scholars Koshan and Hamilton's analysis, Justice Abella's recognition of the intersectionality in Fraser could help in future cases where the intersection of sex and other enumerated or analogous grounds of discrimination is at issue.[258]

Broadly, the majority decision in *Fraser* departed from a strict, "formalistic" approach to assessing disparate impact that had characterized many of the prior unsuccessful cases.[259] As described by Koshan and Hamilton, "Justice Abella's decision methodologically unravels the knots that have made adverse effects claims difficult to prove."[260] The clarifications in *Fraser* demonstrate an expansive interpretation of the context to be considered when examining whether or not a state action adversely affects a particular group, and acknowledges the importance of intersectionality. *Fraser* also positioned

---

[252] Ibid. para 57.
[253] Ibid. at para 59. Here, Justice Abella cites several scholarly works including: Colleen Sheppard, 'Of Forest Fires and Systemic Discrimination: A Review of British Columbia (Public Service Employee Relations Commission) v. BCGSEU' (2001) 46 McGill law journal 533; Vizkelety (n 219); Fredman (n 220).
[254] Grace Ajele and Jena McGill, 'Intersectionality in Law and Legal Contexts' (2020) <https:// www.leaf.ca/publication/intersectionality-in-law-and-legal-contexts/> 4.
[255] Ibid. 45.
[256] *Fraser v. Canada (Attorney General)* (n 220) at para 116.
[257] Ibid. at para 114.
[258] Koshan and Hamilton (n 225) 8.
[259] *Fraser v. Canada (Attorney General)* (n 220) at para 134.
[260] Koshan and Hamilton (n 225) 5.

statistical evidence as a tool to assist in the analysis of the contextual factors, supporting rather than driving that analysis.

We propose standards for the measurement of disparity based on the collective insights discussed in Sections 3.2 and 3.3 above, following a brief discussion of disaggregated data which immediately follows.

3.4 DISAGGREGATED DATA

In order to calculate any measures of disparity, disaggregated data is needed for the characteristics of interest. For example, in the illustrative scenario, if the Agency wanted to estimate the disparity in high risk scores between Black and White applicants, they would have had to have been authorized to collect and analyze applicants' race information. The analysis of race information for the purpose of measuring disparity does not carry the cautions discussed in Chapter 2 of using race or other protected characteristics to build the prediction. The former is meant to mitigate bias and the latter causes bias — a paradox conceptually and practically. Disaggregated data must be analyzed to prevent discrimination, but collecting disaggregated data has been controversial. For example, collecting race data was long overlooked due to "institutionalized denialism,"[261] or was a prohibited practice in order to prevent it from being used unlawfully to apply differential treatment.[262] Race is just one characteristic for which disaggregated data is needed. A comprehensive approach to measuring disparity requires examination across all characteristics protected under the *Charter* — race, national, or ethnic origin, colour, religion, sex, age, or mental or physical disability — and relevant intersections of these characteristics.

The collection of disaggregated data has recently become a focus for governments in Canada. Ontario's *Anti-Racism Data Standards* includes detailed guidance for PSOs regarding methods of data collection at a disaggregated level, an element of Ontario's 3-Year Anti-Racism Strategic Plan, which has mandated the collection of race-based data in child welfare,

---

[261] Grand Chief Stewart Phillip, president of the Union of BC Indian Chiefs as cited in: Government of British Columbia, 'New Anti-Racism Data Act Will Help Fight Systemic Racism' (2022) <https://news.gov.bc.ca/releases/2022PREM0027-000673>.

[262] For detailed analysis of this paradox in the context of machine learning, as well as proposals for legislative and policy reform in the US, see: Xiang (n 216) 666–674; Daniel E Ho and Alice Xiang, 'Affirmative Algorithms: The Legal Grounds for Fairness as Awareness' (2020) <http://arxiv.org/abs/2012.14285>. For the European context, see Fredman (n 220) at Chapter 4.

education and justice sectors by 2023.[263] Other provinces have similarly begun to mandate the collection of disaggregated data,[264] and the Canadian Human Rights Commission's *Anti-Racism Action Plan* has incorporated the collection of race data into its 2021 Data Strategy.[265] In late 2021, Statistics Canada launched its Disaggregated Data Action Plan to expand the collection, access and development of standards related to data and statistical information for a variety of population groups including "women, Indigenous peoples, racialized populations and people living with disabilities."[266]

3.5 CHAPTER SUMMARY: STANDARDS FOR THE MEASUREMENT OF DISPARITY

The purpose of this chapter is to propose standards for the measurement of disparity in ML-based predictions in the context of an ADM system. These standards will help agencies assess whether the degree of disparity observed in predictions suggests disparate impact in the outcome of the administrative decision informed by the prediction.

First, the agency must seek a broad understanding of the social and policy context within which they plan to use ADM, in order to consider how *predictions* used by decision-makers could result in decisions that yield disparate impacts across groups and at their intersections. This is a significant undertaking that includes determining (at minimum) which groups should be compared for disparate impact in the given policy context and why, devising a testing protocol to define and measure disparity across relevant groups, and establishing and justifying what a meaningful difference between groups is.

Second, in alignment with Justice Abella's interpretations in *Fraser*, this testing strategy must be sensitive to the fact that discriminatory effects may not be uniformly felt across members of a defined group, yet could still constitute disparity. Thus, agencies must consider if and how measures of disparity for individuals would be relevant in the policy context, to augment

---

263 Government of Ontario (n 234).

264 See, e.g., legislation proposed in British Columbia in May, 2022: Government of British Columbia, 'Anti-Racism Data Act: About the Legislation' (2022) <https://engage.gov.bc.ca/antiracism/data-act/>.

265 Canadian human rights commission, 'Anti-Racism Action Plan' (2021) <https://www.chrc-ccdp.gc.ca/sites/default/files/2021-09/Anti-Racism Action Plan — September 2021.PDF>. 15

266 Statistics Canada, 'Disaggregated Data Action Plan: Why It Matters To You' (2021) <https://www150.statcan.gc.ca/n1/pub/11-627-m/11-627-m2021092-eng.htm>.

their measures of disparity for identified groups (e.g., adapting suggestions provided in Section 2.4.2).

Third, it is critical that disaggregated data be available for the groups of interest to support this effort — without disaggregated data, it would be impossible to carry out the proposed testing with precision. As acknowledged by scholars and in *Fraser*, however, data for all desired comparisons may not be available and this limitation includes the prospect of lack of disaggregated data. Nonetheless, agencies should seek and use disaggregated data wherever possible.

Further, measures of statistical significance are not sufficient evidence in isolation as a measure of disparate impact. Throughout their efforts to measure disparity, agencies should use qualitative data to validate their understanding of how disparate impact could manifest, regardless of the availability of disaggregated data and measures of statistical significance.

Table 3.1 summarizes the proposed standards for the measurement of disparity.[267] We emphasize that these are not an exhaustive set of standards but an illustrative set meant as a starting point. The standards presented here complement the use of the standards provided in Chapter 2 for the control of algorithmic bias, during the design and development of the ML algorithm before it is put into use. We elaborate on how an agency could adopt and implement these standards, in Chapter 4.

TABLE 3.1   Proposed standards for the measurement of disparity

STANDARDS FOR THE MEASUREMENT OF DISPARITY IN PREDICTIONS
Context-specific definition:
1. Relevant groups and intersections
2. Individual measures
3. Meaningful difference
4. Testing protocol
5. Disaggregated data
6. Qualitative and quantitative data

---

[267] The federal methodology Gender Based Analysis Plus could be used to support the implementation of these standards (see: Government of Canada, 'What Is Gender-Based Analysis Plus' (2022) <https://women-gender-equality.canada.ca/en/gender-based-analysis-plus/what-gender-based-analysis-plus.html>). Notably, the Directive's Algorithmic Impact Assessment includes a question asking whether a "Gender Based Analysis Plus of the data" will be conducted (see section titled "Data Quality" after selecting "Start your assessment" in: Government of Canada, 'Algorithmic Impact Assessment (AIA)' (2023) <https://www.canada.ca/en/government/system/digital-government/digital-government-innovations/responsible-use-ai/algorithmic-impact-assessment.html>). IRCC also recommends the use of this methodology in relation to ADM, see: Immigration Refugees and Citizenship Canada (n 87) 8.

Implementation Recommendations 4

4.1 OVERVIEW OF THE STANDARDS FRAMEWORK

Recall the central question for this work:

> In the context of the Directive, what standards can be derived from legal principles and precedent for the control of algorithmic bias in ML in order to mitigate disparate impact in administrative decisions?

The standards proposed in Chapters 2 and 3 are consolidated in Table 4.1, covering all three stated dimensions for the control of algorithmic bias: standards 1 through 7 cover mitigating the creation of biased predictions; standards 8 and 9 address evaluating predictions for the influence of algorithmic bias; and standards 10 through 15 focus on measuring disparity in predictions. Taken together, these standards comprise a framework for agencies seeking to control algorithmic bias in order to mitigate the outcome of disparate impact in their decisions.

Aside from being an organized collection of standards, framework here means a package that is not divisible to its individual elements. This framework provides a starting point for inspection and testing, expanding upon the requirements already present in the Directive. Agencies must consider the full scope of the proposed standards framework and determine what is relevant to the policy context. Our work is illustrative rather than exhaustive and agencies are thus encouraged to consider additional standards relevant to their policy context. However, agencies should not neglect any of the standards proposed here because our work has shown these standards to be integral to the task of fair decision-making and the mitigation of disparate impact, based both on ML research and based upon the law.

DOI: 10.1201/b23364-4

TABLE 4.1 Standards framework for the control of algorithmic bias

STANDARDS TO MITIGATE THE CREATION OF BIASED PREDICTIONS

Overall:
  1. Construct validity
  2. Knowledge limits

Model input data (spanning personal and non-personal information):
  3. Accuracy and provenance
  4. Measurement validity
  5. Representativeness

Model target of prediction:
  6. Measurement validity
  7. Match to policy objective

STANDARDS FOR THE EVALUATION OF PREDICTIONS
8. Uncertainty
9. Individual fairness
STANDARDS FOR THE MEASUREMENT OF DISPARITY IN PREDICTIONS
Context-specific definition: 10. Relevant groups and intersections 11. Individual measures 12. Meaningful difference
13. Testing protocol
14. Disaggregated data
15. Qualitative and quantitative data

The standards proposed here are also consistent with the expected evolution of the Directive. TBS performs a review of the Directive every six months, the most recently published review, at the time of writing, being its third review dated Winter 2022 (3rd review) whose objective is stated as:

> The 3rd review of the Treasury Board Directive on Automated Decision-Making takes stock of the current state of the policy instrument and identifies several risks and challenges to the federal government's commitment to responsible artificial intelligence (AI). It discusses critical gaps that limit the Directive's relevance and effectiveness in supporting transparency, accountability, and fairness in automated decision-making.[268]

At the time of writing, no policy update has yet been issued for the Directive based on the 3rd review; however, it is notable that the 3rd review

---

[268] Bitar, Deshaies, and Hall (n 169) 2.

identified policy recommendations that align with the standards we have proposed for the control of algorithmic bias (and none of the recommendations conflict with any of the standards proposed here). For example, the recommendation is made to "Expand the pre-production testing requirement to cover model bias testing."[269] This entire work is aligned with this recommendation, and the standards we have proposed build out the details needed to support the practical implementation of this recommendation. Additionally, a recommendation is made for the:

> Addition of new subsection under section 6.3 titled "**Data Governance**": "**Establishing measures to ensure that data used and generated by the Automated Decision System are traceable, protected, and appropriately retained and disposed of in accordance with the Directive on Service and Digital, Directive on Privacy Practices, and Directive on Security Management.**"[270]

Traceability for data aligns with standard 3 for provenance of input data. These TBS recommendations demonstrate the federal government's continued commitment to the control of algorithmic bias for fair and rational decision-making in the administrative context. Yet much work remains for agencies to implement the Directive's current (and recommended) requirements. We believe the standards framework presented here can make a contribution to this effort, and in the remainder of this chapter, we provide several recommendations for implementation.

4.2 IMPLEMENTING THE STANDARDS FRAMEWORK

First, we must emphasize that this standards framework is *solely directed towards the control of algorithmic bias* in order to mitigate disparate impact. Accordingly, this framework would comprise only a subset of an agency's overall approach to the use of ADM in a way that is compliant with the Directive and so that fair and reasonable decisions result. IRCC's Policy Playbook, referenced throughout this work, provides an excellent example of what a comprehensive approach to the use of ADM would entail, including

---

[269] Ibid. 20.
[270] Ibid. 21 (emphasis is original).

(but not limited to) items such as guiding principles aligned with agency objectives; general suitability criteria for ADM in the policy context; agency training and staffing considerations; necessary privacy and legal assessments; stakeholder, partner, and public engagement; transparency and accountability requirements; and, system security controls.[271] The proposed standards framework for the control of algorithmic bias cannot be implemented in isolation — it must be situated within, and cohere with, the agency's holistic approach to ADM. The standards we have proposed here have been stated generically, and they can only be made specific and actionable when they are adapted to the policy and decision-making context to which ADM is being applied.

Adapting standards to the policy context can be done in a way that is very stringent where requirements and thresholds are put in place that offer little room to manoeuvre, or standards can be more loosely applied. Whatever approach the agency takes to standards to control algorithmic bias will affect the quality of the decisions and outcomes being made and may involve trade-offs with other technical factors such as predictive accuracy.[272] Algorithmic bias is not a binary characteristic, it is a matter of degree, and it is typically difficult or impossible to eliminate algorithmic bias altogether. A whole domain of ML research and practice has sprung up to define mathematical fairness metrics and other statistical methods that could be used to support the implementation of the proposed standards, although the practical applicability of these methods remains under investigation.[273] In short, controlling algorithmic bias is not black and white. It is a balancing exercise that is part statistics, part policy analysis, part legislative interpretation, part stakeholder consultation, and — perhaps most importantly in the administrative context — it is in large part a consideration of Daly's four dimensions of justification (reasoned decision-making, responsiveness, demonstrated expertise, and contextualism). Standards are the "how" that respond to the "what" contained in the four dimensions of justification.

Further, as described in Section 2.1.3, the principle of proportionality is fundamental in the administrative context. To this end, the Directive mandates that an Algorithmic Impact Assessment be performed by all agencies using ADM, which consists of a questionnaire that assesses the impact of ADM on "the rights, health and economic interests of individuals, entities

---

[271] Immigration Refugees and Citizenship Canada (n 87).

[272] See, e.g., discussion of fairness-accuracy trade-off in Friedler and others (n 216).

[273] See, e.g., Kroll and others (n 86) 687–690. See also Friedler and others (n 216); Sam Corbett-Davies and Sharad Goel, 'The Measure and Mismeasure of Fairness: A Critical Review of Fair Machine Learning' (2018) <http://arxiv.org/abs/1808.00023>; International Organization for Standardization (n 81) 14–27; Xiang (n 216). Section VII.

or communities, and/or the ongoing sustainability of an ecosystem."[274] The Directive then references specific procedural requirements (including peer review, notice, human-in-the-loop, explanation, testing, monitoring, training, contingency planning, and approval) that are scaled according to impact level, with greater procedural safeguards required at higher levels of impact.[275] Notably, the Directive does not scale its existing requirements for pre-production testing for data biases according to level of impact, nor is there any evidence that the proposed expansion of the scope of testing for model bias referenced in the 3rd review would be scaled according to level of impact. We strongly recommend, however, that the assessed level of impact of the ADM system be used to inform the implementation of controls for algorithmic bias, thereby incorporating the principle of proportionality into practical application, i.e., decisions with greater impact should be subject to more stringent application of standards and thresholds.[276]

Even though the proposed standards apply to activities taking place during the design, development, and testing of the algorithm, that does not mean that the perspectives of designers and developers alone are sufficient to determine precisely how the standards should be adapted for the given policy context. The IRCC Playbook lists 13 distinct groups of subject matter experts internal to government that should be considered when undertaking an ADM system.[277] For the work of controlling bias, NIST strongly recommends multistakeholder engagement,[278] and ISO highlights the need for a diverse team consisting of individuals with expertise from a variety of disciplines including:

- social scientists and ethics specialists;
- data scientists and quality specialists;
- legal and data privacy experts;
- representatives of users or groups of external stakeholders.[279]

---

[274] Government of Canada, 'Algorithmic Impact Assessment Tool' (2022) <https://www.canada.ca/en/government/system/digital-government/digital-government-innovations/responsible-use-ai/algorithmic-impact-assessment.html>.

[275] Government of Canada Treasury Board Secretariat, 'Directive on Automated Decision-Making' (n 1). Appendix C — Impact Level Requirements.

[276] In the context of technology-assisted administrative decision-making, Daly discussed the contrast between decisions characterized as leaning to the "political" (because they entail a "broad range of rational outcomes") compared to those characterized leaning to the "legal" (with a "narrow range of rational outcomes"), suggesting requirements for fairness could differ across this spectrum. See: Daly (n 88). 14–15. How Daly's approach intersects with the Directive's impact assessment could be a fruitful area of research to further evolve the impact assessment methodology.

[277] Immigration Refugees and Citizenship Canada (n 87). 11–13

[278] Schwartz and others (n 66) 46.

[279] International Organization for Standardization (n 81) 19.

This point cannot be overstated and it is imperative that all agencies implementing the standards framework engage broad and diverse perspectives. The standards framework is for use in the design and development of the algorithm, before is deployed by the agency to assist the decision-maker. The testing protocol for the measurement of disparity in standard 13 is pre-deployment testing. Design, development, and pre-deployment testing refer generically to stages in a project or application lifecycle, and agencies will have a specific lifecycle paradigm they are working within. IRCC, for example, references a five-stage AI Project Lifecycle spanning diagnostics, design, development, testing, record keeping, client communication and maintenance.[280] The project lifecycle will typically specify roles and responsibilities for carrying out activities at each stage, requiring the broad and diverse perspectives described earlier. It will also typically indicate decision points throughout the lifecycle — gates for which certain criteria must be met in order for the work to proceed. The proposed standards will be particularly helpful in informing the gating criteria. For example, consider that a threshold or acceptable range for uncertainty (standard 8) has been specified as appropriate for a particular decision-making context, and to be assessed as part of a testing stage. If the uncertainty ascertained during testing does not meet the stated threshold or is not within the acceptable range, then the agency may choose to suspend deployment of the algorithm, until improvements can be made. The overall ADM approach may include multiple gates such as this, which illustrates the value of the standards framework: translating the concepts of algorithmic bias into measurable criteria that are assessed prior to deployment, to ensure that ADM will result in decisions that are fair to those impacted by them.

Finally, and in reference to the need for evidence in Daly's third dimension of justification — demonstrated expertise — agencies should fully document both the "what" and "why" of their efforts to implement the standards framework in any given policy context. This would include not only the operational aspects of ADM (i.e., thresholds, gates, diverse participation, etc., as described earlier) but also the actual decisions that decision-makers arrived at, and how the ADM predictions shaped their decisions. Documentation supports the ongoing monitoring and improvement of the agency's use of ADM, and is also important evidence of the agency's demonstrated expertise.

It is possible that our readers still have questions on how to implement the standards framework. We have presented a preliminary recommendation for implementing the fifteen proposed standards in the framework, not a step-by-step recipe for implementation of each standard. That is because

---

[280] Immigration Refugees and Citizenship Canada (n 87) 37.

such a recipe does not exist. The standards framework is soft law at a very high level, presented as a starting point. Agencies must do the hard work of interpreting and adapting the proposed standards within their policy and decision-making context, deriving more specific contextualized standards and supporting processes, and embedding these into their project lifecycles. Implementation of these specific standards and supporting processes will typically require a period of trial and adjustment, within an overall change management methodology.

Applying the discussion in Section 2.1.2 of soft law in practice to standards, this also requires (at least) that the people developing and using standards are sufficiently trained; that standards support rather than unduly limit the discretion of decision-makers; that institutional practices reinforce the policy aims that the standards are directed towards; and, that the technological systems through which standards are implemented are fit for purpose. If soft-law standards are the bricks, the aforementioned factors (training, discretion, institutional practices, and technological systems) are the scaffolding — both of which are needed to raise a building, and both of which are fair game for judicial scrutiny in complaints. Agencies using ADM must invest in the development and implementation of standards to control algorithmic bias in order to make fair and rational decisions now, and to position themselves for judicial deference should it become needed in future.

Conclusions and Further Research

5

We began this work by discussing the EU AIA draft legislation, now undergoing parliamentary review prior to its enactment which is expected to take place in 2023 or 2024.[281] The EU AIA states goals for the protection of fundamental rights as well as for the creation of a single regulated EU market for AI systems. The prominence of rights protection in the EU AIA is not surprising, given the many rights infringements implicated by AI that have been documented in a wide variety of applications across the world. References to standards appear throughout the EU AIA where they are put forward as a means for the protection of fundamental rights, however many questions remain as to whether SDOs are equipped for the task of developing appropriate standards for this objective.

By contrast, the Directive — Canada's federal policy applicable to ADM in the administrative context — contains no explicit mention of standards or rights protections in its text, but is inherently subject to the principles of administrative law and bound to uphold the rights guaranteed in the *Charter*. This structural contrast prompted us to ask if and how standards could be put in place to protect human rights in the context of the Directive. We illustrated how SDOs, today, typically approach standards for AI and ADM as solutions to particular technical problems. We then built upon the work of scholars from diverse domains to argue that the starting point for standards should instead be the norms encapsulated by law, and that when integrated with a technical understanding of ML that underlies ADM, the law would illuminate important areas for standards. We used case study and literature review to illustrate how statistical and computational aspects of algorithmic bias

---

[281] Laura De Boel, 'Council of the EU Proposes Amendments to Draft AI Act' (2022) <https://www.wsgr.com/en/insights/council-of-the-eu-proposes-amendments-to-draft-ai-act.html#:~:text=They are expected to vote,to-three years to comply.>.

produce disparate impact in ML-based predictions, shaping the final central question of this work:

> In the context of the Directive, what standards can be derived from legal principles and precedent for the control of algorithmic bias in ML in order to mitigate disparate impact in administrative decisions?

In Chapter 2, we explored administrative law and the culture of justification in depth, identifying the principles of reasonableness (and indicia of unreasonableness) in substantive review to inform standards. We also addressed points of intersection between the Directive and privacy law, that are relevant to algorithmic bias. Throughout Chapter 2, we drew heavily from, and expanded upon, the interdisciplinary work spanning law and ML of several US and European scholars. Chapter 2 yielded seven proposed standards to mitigate the creation of biased predictions (construct validity; knowledge limits; accuracy and provenance, measurement validity, and representativeness in input data; measurement validity and match to policy objective for the target of prediction) and two proposed standards for the evaluation of predictions for the influence of algorithmic bias (uncertainty and individual fairness).

In Chapter 3, we confronted the persistent challenge of the measurement of disparity, and proposed a modern approach from which to derive standards based on the recent SCC decision in *Fraser*. We also explained the importance and role of disaggregated data in mitigating disparate impact. The analysis in Chapter 3 yielded six proposed standards for the measurement of disparity, covering: context-specific definitions of relevant groups and intersections, individual measures and what entails a meaningful difference; testing protocol; disaggregated data; and, qualitative and quantitative data.

In Chapter 4, we consolidated all the standards proposed into a framework, describing the characteristics of the framework and providing recommendations for the successful implementation of the standards by agencies using ADM. Central to these recommendations is adapting the standards to the specific policy and decision-making context: a multidisciplinary exercise in balance. In Chapter 4, we also reinforced factors leading to the effective implementation of soft law. Referencing the most recent review of the Directive by TBS, we showed our proposed standards to be well-aligned with the Directive and its planned updates.

The main conclusion is straightforward: Yes, standards *can* be derived from legal principles and precedent for the control of algorithmic bias in order to mitigate disparate impact in administrative decisions. This work is important because it contributes in a tangible and actionable way to fair and justifiable administrative decisions using ADM. It is our hope that the standards framework will help more agencies build and deploy ADM with confidence that they will not be risking rights infringements, for the benefit of government and their clients alike.

This work also demonstrates the value of multidisciplinary work: rather than standards derived from either a technical or a legal domain, the standards proposed here sit at the intersection of both. This could mean they are better substantiated versus those derived within the worldview of only one domain. We have also developed and demonstrated a methodology that can be used to locate a space of agreement between the two domains, i.e., agreement on the factors contributing to algorithmic bias that need to be controlled. This methodology — that begins with the law, and then weaves in relevant technical strands — could be extended beyond the scope of the standards proposed in this work, to identify standards for other stages in the AI lifecycle or for other objectives than mitigation of disparate impact. This multidisciplinary methodology could also help stakeholders from diverse professional backgrounds understand and implement the standards.

Further, the standards framework proposed here makes a tangible contribution to Hadfield's vision of justifiable AI, discussed in Section 1.5. In contrast to the mainly technical notions of XAI, justifiable AI demands that those impacted by decisions using AI (including ADM) be able to understand the factors used in coming to a decision about them, and that those factors should be based first and foremost on legal and societal norms. This work contributes to both of these objectives: the specific standards proposed have conceptually accessible meanings that could be used to support reasons for decisions, and all of the standards have been derived from law.

What are the implications of this work? First, the clear operational implication for agencies planning to use ADM is that they must put tremendous focus on the quality of the predictions they use to inform decision-makers, and will have to become experts at measuring disparity. This is the reality unless they wish to risk making unfair (and possibly unlawful) decisions, and unless they wish to invite scrutiny by a reviewing court should their decisions come under judicial review. Implementing the proposed standards framework, taking into consideration the recommendations provided, is a starting point. At the same time, doing so is clearly a major undertaking for any agency, and as such, the use case for ADM will have to be one with a clear benefit, given the work that must be done to implement the standards and recommendations described here. For agencies that do choose to implement a standards framework such as the one we have proposed here, justification of ML-based ADM is within reach and those agencies can be confident that they are actively controlling for important factors that lead to disparate impact.

Second, and in keeping with government commitments to public transparency, TBS and administrative bodies using ADM should also consider whether standards such as those proposed here, and other relevant standards, should be made publicly available. Doing so could increase public trust in government use of ADM — building on Daly's "social acceptability" concept discussed in Section 1.5. We ask our readers: If an administrative decision with some meaningful impact to *you* is made using ADM, would knowing that the agency had implemented standards such as those proposed here, to ensure that the decision made was fair, lawful and justifiable, build your trust in government? The answer is yes for us and we hope our readers can say the same.

Clear and actionable standards have been proposed here that align well with the TBS planned policy updates to mitigate model bias. TBS should examine these standards and implementation recommendations; consider formalizing the role and function of standards, such as those proposed here, in the Directive itself, in supporting policies, or in their supplementary guidance to agencies; and, TBS should provide support to agencies in the use of these standards. Implementing the standards proposed here provides a mechanism to hold decision-makers accountable for making fair and unbiased decisions in their use of ADM, the third and perhaps most important implication of this work.

This work motivates much additional study, including changes in the law that may be needed to respond to unique challenges of AI and ADM (as discussed in Sections 1.5 and 2.4.2). Additionally, the scope of this work was deliberately narrow: i.e., it addressed only: statistical and computational factors of algorithmic bias; ADM that assists versus being fully determinative of a decision; and, a very specific focus on the outcome of disparate impact as relates to the *Charter* guarantee of substantive equality. The standards proposed here were illustrative and non-exhaustive, meant as a starting point. Any and all of these scope limitations could be opened up for further research, still within the context of the Directive. The standards proposed here were not specific to any industry sector or application — research that delivers standards tailored to a specific problem area could prove to be accelerators for innovation.

In proposing standards for the measurement of disparity, we briefly mentioned that intersectionality should be addressed, but we did not elaborate on the analysis needed to do so or what more detailed standards relating to intersectionality could look like. This would be a fruitful area for further interdisciplinary work. Similarly, throughout this work, we drew from the existing body of technical work on algorithmic bias to inform my proposed standards, but did not extend any of the technical solutions to better respond to the standards. Further work could be done to produce technical solutions optimized for the proposed standards.

Finally, further research should be directed to answering the many very salient questions stemming from the fact that the Directive is a policy, compared with the EU AIA and other legislative proposals emerging around the world for the regulation of AI. Such work could examine how the reach, scope, enforcement, effectiveness, flexibility, longevity, public perception, trade implications and so much more differ across these different approaches and instruments for regulation.

References

AI Now, 'Automated Decision Systems: Examples of Government Use Cases' (2019) <https://ainowinstitute.org/nycadschart.pdf>

Ajele, G and McGill, J, 'Intersectionality in Law and Legal Contexts' (2020) <https://www.leaf.ca/publication/intersectionality-in-law-and-legal-contexts/> 4, 45

AlgorithmWatch, 'Automating Society Report 2020' (2020) <https://algorithmwatch.org/en/automating-society-2020/> 7

——, 'Draft AI Act: EU Needs to Live up to Its Own Ambitions in Terms of Governance and Enforcement' (2021) <https://algorithmwatch.org/en/eu-ai-actconsultation-submission-2021/#:~:text=Newsletters-,Draft AI Act%3A EU needs to live up to its, transparency requirements and enforcement mechanisms> 5–6

Alkhatib, A, 'To Live in Their Utopia: Why Algorithmic Systems Create Absurd Outcomes', *CHI Conference on Human Factors in Computing Systems (CHI '21), May 8–13, 2021, Yokohama, Japan.* (ACM 2021) 9

Alston, P, 'Report of the Special Rapporteur on Extreme Poverty and Human Rights A/74/493' (2019) <https://undocs.org/A/74/493> 11

Angwin, J and others, 'Machine Bias' (*ProPublica*, 2016) <https://www.propublica.org/article/machine-bias-risk-assessments-in-criminal-sentencing>

Babbie, ER, *The Practice of Social Research* (13th ed., Wadsworth Cengage Learning 2013) 132, 191–192

Babuta, A and Oswald, M, 'Data Analytics and Algorithmic Bias in Policing' (2019) <https://assets.publishing.service.gov.uk/government/uploads/system/uploads/attachment_data/file/831750/RUSI_Report_-_Algorithms_and_Bias_in_Policing.pdf>

Baker, S, 'The Flawed Claims About Bias in Facial Recognition' (*Lawfare*, 2022) <https://www.lawfareblog.com/flawed-claims-about-bias-facial-recognition>

Barocas, S and Selbst, AD, 'Big Data's Disparate Impact' (2016) 104 California Law Review 671, 688

Bitar, O, Deshaies, B and Hall, D, '3rd Review of the Treasury Board Directive on Automated Decision-Making' (2022) SSRN Electronic Journal <https://www.ssrn.com/abstract=4087546> 2, 7, 20–21

Boddington, P, 'Normative Modes: Codes and Standards', *Oxford Handbook of Ethics of AI* (Oxford University Press 2020) 130

Braun, E, 'Adverse Effect Discrimination: Proving the Prima Facie Case' (2005) 11 Review of Constitutional Studies 119, 125–127, 129–131

Browne, KR, 'Statistical Proof of Discrimination: Beyond "Damned Lies."' (1993) 68 Washington Law Review

Canadian Human Rights Commission, 'Anti-Racism Action Plan' (2021) <https://www.chrc-ccdp.gc.ca/sites/default/files/2021-09/Anti-Racism Action Plan – September 2021.PDF> 15

Centre for Data Ethics and Innovation, 'Review into Bias in Algorithmic Decision-Making' (2020) <https://www.gov.uk/government/publications/cdei-publishes-review-into-bias-in-algorithmic-decision-making>

Chouldechova, A and Roth, A, 'A Snapshot of the Frontiers of Fairness in Machine Learning' (2020) 63(5) Communications of the ACM. 85

Christian, B, *The Alignment Problem* (W W Norton & Company Inc 2020) 65, 277–310

Citron, DK and Pasquale, FA, 'The Scored Society: Due Process for Automated Predictions' (2014) 89(1) Washington Law Review 24

Cobbe, J, 'Administrative Law and the Machines of Government: Judicial Review of Automated Public-Sector Decision-Making' (2019) 39 Legal Studies 639–640, 651, 653

Cobbe, J, Lee, MSA and Singh, J, 'Reviewable Automated Decision-Making', *Proceedings of the 2021 ACM Conference on Fairness, Accountability, and Transparency* (ACM 2021) <https://dl.acm.org/doi/10.1145/3442188.3445921>

Coglianese, C, 'A Framework for Governmental Use of Machine Learning' (2020) <https://www.acus.gov/sites/default/files/documents/Coglianese ACUS Final Report w Cover Page.pdf> 40, 45, 58, 66–69

Coglianese, C and Lehr, D, 'Transparency and Algorithmic Governance' (2019) 71 Administrative Law Review 1, 7, 13–14, 20, 34–36

Corbett-Davies, S and Goel, S, 'The Measure and Mismeasure of Fairness: A Critical Review of Fair Machine Learning' <http://arxiv.org/abs/1808.00023> 17

Council of Europe Commissioner for Human Rights, 'Unboxing Artificial Intelligence: 10 Steps to Protect Human Rights' (2019) <https://www.coe.int/en/web/commissioner/-/unboxing-artificial-intelligence-10-steps-to-protect-human-rights> 24

Council of Europe Committee of Experts on Internet Intermediaries (MSI-NET), 'Study on the Human Rights Dimensions of Automated Data Processing Techniques (In Particular Algorithms) and Possible Regulatory Implications.' (2018) <https://edoc.coe.int/en/internet/7589-algorithms-and-human-rights-study-on-the-human-rights-dimensions-of-automated-data-processing-techniques-and-possible-regulatory-implications.html>

'Criminal Law – Sentencing Guidelines – Wisconsin Supreme Court Requires Warning before Use of Algorithmic Risk Assessments in Sentencing – State v. Loomis. (Case Note)' (2017) 130 Harvard Law Review. < https://harvardlawreview.org/2017/03/state-v-loomis/#:~:text=the%20Wisconsin%20Supreme%20Court%20held,court%20nor%20to%20the%20defendant> 1530

Cumming, S and Caragata, L, 'Rationing "Rights": Supplementary Welfare Benefits and Lone Moms' (2011) 12 Critical Social Work <https://ojs.uwindsor.ca/index.php/csw/article/view/5844> 82

Daly, P, 'Artificial Administration: Administrative Law in the Age of Machines' (2019) SSRN Electronic Journal <https://www.ssrn.com/abstract=3493381> 7, 13–15, 16–18, 21–23

———, 'Vavilov and the Culture of Justification in Contemporary Administrative Law' (2021) 100 The Supreme Court Law Review: Osgoode's Annual Constitutional Cases Conference 279, 281–290

Danks, D, 'Learning' in Keith Frankish and William M Ramsey (eds), *The Cambridge Handbook of Artificial Intelligence* (Cambridge University Press 2014) 158

Danks, D and London, AJ, 'Algorithmic Bias in Autonomous Systems', *Proceedings of the Twenty-Sixth International Joint Conference on Artificial Intelligence (IJCAI-17)* (2017) <https://www.researchgate.net/profile/Alex-London/publication/318830422_Algorithmic_Bias_in_Autonomous_Systems/links/5a4bb017aca2729b7c893d1b/Algorithmic-Bias-in-Autonomous-Systems.pdf> 1491

Davis, KC, *Discretionary Justice; A Preliminary Inquiry* (Louisiana State University Press 1969)

De Boel, L, 'Council of the EU Proposes Amendments to Draft AI Act' (2022) <https://www.wsgr.com/en/insights/council-of-the-eu-proposes-amendments-to-draft-ai-act.html#:~:text=They are expected to vote,to-three years to comply>

Dong, G and Liu, H, *Feature Engineering for Machine Learning and Data Analytics* (CRC Press 2018)

Doshi-Velez, F and Kim, B, 'Towards A Rigorous Science of Interpretable Machine Learning' <https://arxiv.org/abs/1702.08608>

Eliadis, P, *Speaking Out on Human Rights: Debating Canada's Human Rights System* (MQUP 2014) Appendix Three

Engstrom, DF and others, 'Government by Algorithm: Artificial Intelligence in Federal Administrative Agencies' (2020) <https://www-cdn.law.stanford.edu/wp-content/uploads/2020/02/ACUS-AI-Report.pdf> 21–69

Engstrom, DF and Ho, DE, 'Algorithmic Accountability in the Administrative State' (2020) 37 Yale Journal on Regulation 800, 833, 839

Equifax Inc., 'How Are Credit Scores Calculated?' (2022) <https://www.equifax.com/personal/education/credit/score/how-is-credit-score-calculated/>

Eubanks, V, *Automating Inequality* (St Martin's Press 2017)

European Commission Directorate-General for Employment Social Affairs and Inclusion, 'Comparative Study on the Collection of Data to Measure the Extent and Impact of Discrimination within the United States, Canada, Australia, the United Kingdom and the Netherlands' (2004) <https://op.europa.eu/en/publication-detail/-/publication/cedfe9eb-9be9-4697-b7be-0551c2523140/language-en> 40–41, 48–79

European Digital Rights (EDRi) and others, 'An EU Artificial Intelligence Act for Fundamental Rights: A Civil Society Statement' (2021) <https://algorithmwatch.org/en/eu-artificial-intelligence-act-for-fundamental-rights/#:~:text=The EU's Artificial Intelligence Act,is set out to achieve> 4

Finck, M, 'Automated Decision-Making and Administrative Law' in Peter Cane and others (eds), *Oxford Handbook of Comparative Administrative Law* (Oxford University Press 2020)

Flood, CM and Dolling, J, 'A Historical Map for Administrative Law: There Be Dragons' in Colleen M Flood and Lorne Sossin (eds), *Administrative Law in Context* (Third, Emond Montgomery Publications Limited 2018) 3

Fox-Decent, E and Pless, A, 'The Charter and Administrative Law Part I: Procedural Fairness' in Colleen M Flood and Lorne Sossin (eds), *Administrative Law in Context* (Third, Emond Montgomery Publications Limited 2018) 245, 246

Fredman, S, *Discrimination Law* (2nd ed., Oxford University Press 2011) 153–231

Friedler, SA and others, 'A Comparative Study of Fairness-Enhancing Interventions in Machine Learning', *Proceedings of the Conference on Fairness, Accountability, and Transparency* (ACM 2019) <https://dl.acm.org/doi/10.1145/3287560.3287589>

Friedler, SA, Scheidegger, C and Venkatasubramanian, S, 'On the (Im)Possibility of Fairness' <http://arxiv.org/abs/1609.07236>

Future of Life Institute, 'The AI Act: Developments' (2022) <https://artificialintel
ligenceact.eu/developments/>

Geist, M, 'AI and International Regulation' in Florian Martin-Bariteau and Teresa
Scassa (eds), *Artificial Intelligence and the Law in Canada* (LexisNexis
Canada Inc 2021) 370–373

Government of British Columbia, 'Anti-Racism Data Act: About the Legislation'
(2022) <https://engage.gov.bc.ca/antiracism/data-act/>

——, 'New Anti-Racism Data Act Will Help Fight Systemic Racism' (2022)
<https://news.gov.bc.ca/releases/2022PREM0027-000673>

Government of Canada, 'Algorithmic Impact Assessment Tool' (2023) <https://www.
canada.ca/en/government/system/digital-government/digital-government-
innovations/responsible-use-ai/algorithmic-impact-assessment.html>

——, 'Employment Equity in the Public Service of Canada for Fiscal Year 2019
to 2020' <https://www.canada.ca/en/government/publicservice/wellness-
inclusion-diversity-public-service/diversity-inclusion-public-service/employment-
equity-annual-reports/employment-equity-public-service-canada-2019-
2020.html>

——, 'Government of Canada Digital Standards: Playbook' (2018) <https://www.
canada.ca/en/government/system/digital-government/government-canada-
digital-standards.html>

——, 'Citizenship: Natural Justice and Procedural Fairness' (2015) <https://
www.canada.ca/en/immigration-refugees-citizenship/corporate/publications-
manuals/operational-bulletins-manuals/canadian-citizenship/admininistration/
decisions/natural-justice-procedural-fairness.html>

——, 'Employment Equity Act: Annual Report 2020' (2020) <https://www.
canada.ca/en/employment-social-development/corporate/portfolio/labour/
programs/employment-equity/reports/2020-annual.html>

——, 'Guideline on Service and Digital' (2023) <https://www.canada.ca/en/
government/system/digital-government/guideline-service-digital.html#ToC4>
Section 4.5.3

——, 'Open Government Portal: Algorithmic Impact Assessment' (2022) <https://
search.open.canada.ca/opendata/?search_text=algorithmic+impact+assessment>

——'Report to the Clerk of the Privy Council: A Data Strategy Roadmap for
the Federal Public Service' (2018) <https://www.canada.ca/en/privy-council/
corporate/clerk/publications/data-strategy.html>

——, 'Responsible Use of Artificial Intelligence (AI): Exploring the Future of
Responsible AI in Government' (2021) <https://www.canada.ca/en/government/
system/digital-government/digital-government-innovations/responsible-use-ai.
html>

——, 'Transparency – ESDC' (2020) <https://www.canada.ca/en/employment-
social-development/corporate/transparency.html>

——, 'What Is Gender-Based Analysis Plus' (2022) <https://women-gender-
equality.canada.ca/en/gender-based-analysis-plus/what-gender-based-analysis-
plus.html>

Government of Canada Department of Justice, 'Section 15 – Equality Rights'
(*Charterpedia*, 2022) <https://www.justice.gc.ca/eng/csj-sjc/rfc-dlc/ccrf-ccdl/
check/art15.html>

————, 'Modernizing Canada's Privacy Act: Online Public Consultation Discussion Paper' (2020) <https://www.justice.gc.ca/eng/csj-sjc/pa-lprp/dp-dd/raa-rar.html> Government of Canada Treasury Board Secretariat, 'Directive on Automated Decision-Making' (2021) <https://www.tbs-sct.gc.ca/pol/doc-eng.aspx?id=32592>

————, 'Policy on Service and Digital' (2019) <https://www.tbs-sct.gc.ca/pol/doc-eng.aspx?id=32603>

Government of Ontario, 'Data Standards for the Identification and Monitoring of Systemic Racism' (2020) <https://www.ontario.ca/document/data-standards-identification-and-monitoring-systemic-racism>

Green, A, 'Delegation and Consultation: How the Administrative State Functions and the Importance of Rules' in Colleen M Flood and Lorne Sossin (eds), *Administrative Law in Context* (Emond Montgomery Publications Limited 2018) 313, 327, 334

Hadfield, GK, 'Explanation and Justification: AI Decision-Making, Law, and the Rights of Citizens' (2021) <https://srinstitute.utoronto.ca/news/hadfield-justifiable-ai>

Hallinan, D and Borgesius, FZ, 'Opinions Can Be Incorrect (in Our Opinion)! On Data Protection Law's Accuracy Principle' (2020) 10 International Data Privacy Law 1 <https://academic.oup.com/idpl/article/10/1/1/5717390>

Hamilton, JW, 'Cautious Optimism: Fraser v Canada (Attorney General)' (2021) 30 Constitutional Forum/Forum Constitutionnel 1, 3–10

Hermstrüwer, Y, 'Artificial Intelligence and Administrative Decisions Under Uncertainty', *Regulating Artificial Intelligence* (Springer International Publishing 2020) 202, 204, 207, 212

Ho, DE and Xiang, A, 'Affirmative Algorithms: The Legal Grounds for Fairness as Awareness' <http://arxiv.org/abs/2012.14285>

Hüllermeier, E and Waegeman, W, 'Aleatoric and Epistemic Uncertainty in Machine Learning: An Introduction to Concepts and Methods' (2021) 110 Machine Learning 457, 458

IEEE, 'IEEE Standards' (2021) <https://www.ieee.org/standards/index.html>

IEEE Standards Organization, 'P7003 – Algorithmic Bias Considerations: Project Details' (2021) <https://standards.ieee.org/project/7003.html>

Immigration Refugees and Citizenship Canada, 'Policy Playbook for Automated Support for Decision-Making' (2021) <https://gccollab.ca/groups/profile/7211943/enircc-digital-policy-guidancefrorientation-stratu00e9gique-du2019ircc-sur-le-numu00e9rique> 7, 8, 11–13, 33, 37

International Organization for Standardization, 'ISO in Brief' (2019) <https://www.iso.org/files/live/sites/isoorg/files/store/en/PUB100007.pdf> 3

————, 'ISO/IEC DTR 24027 Information Technology — Artificial Intelligence (AI) — Bias in AI Systems and AI Aided Decision Making' (2021) <https://www.iso.org/standard/77607.html?browse=tc> 10–13, 14–27

'Interview with Benoit Deshaies, Director, Data and Artificial Intelligence, Office of the Chief Information Officer, Treasury Board of Canada Secretariat, Government of Canada (Toronto, Canada, 27 November 2020)'

'Interview with Gerlinde Weger, Director, Member of the IEEE P7003™ Working Group (Toronto, Canada, 26 April 2021).'

Jacobs, L, 'The Dynamics of Independence, Impartiality, and Bias in the Canadian Administrative State' in Colleen M Flood and Lorne Sossin (eds), *Administrative Law in Context* (Third, Emond Montgomery Publications Limited 2018) 280

Jobin, A, Ienca, M and Vayena, E, 'The Global Landscape of AI Ethics Guidelines' (2019) 1 Nature Machine Intelligence 389 <http://www.nature.com/articles/s42256-019-0088-2> 1

Koene, A, Dowthwaite, L and Seth, S, 'IEEE P7003™ Standard for Algorithmic Bias Considerations', *Proceedings of the International Workshop on Software Fairness* (ACM 2018) <https://dl.acm.org/doi/10.1145/3194770.3194773> 39

Koshan, J and Hamilton, JW, 'Tugging at the Strands: Adverse Effects Discrimination and the Supreme Court Decision in Fraser' (2020) <https://ablawg.ca/2020/11/09/tugging-at-the-strands-adverse-effects-discrimination-and-the-supreme-court-decision-in-fraser/> 5, 8–10

Kroll, JA and others, 'Accountable Algorithms' (2017) 165 The University of Pennsylvania Law Review 633, 642, 656–657, 687–690, 695–696

Kuttner, TS, 'Administrative Tribunals in Canada' (*The Canadian Encyclopedia*, 2020) <https://www.thecanadianencyclopedia.ca/en/article/administrative-tribunals#:~:text=Tribunals are set up by,between people and the government>

Kuziemski, M and Misuraca, G, 'AI Governance in the Public Sector: Three Tales from the Frontiers of Automated Decision-Making in Democratic Settings' (2020) 44 Telecommunications Policy 101976 <https://linkinghub.elsevier.com/retrieve/pii/S0308596120300689>

Larson, J and others, 'How We Analyzed the COMPAS Recidivism Algorithm' (*ProPublica*, 2016) <https://www.propublica.org/article/how-we-analyzed-the-compas-recidivism-algorithm>

Law Commission of Ontario, 'Comparing European and Canadian AI Regulation' (2021) <https://www.lco-cdo.org/wp-content/uploads/2021/12/Comparing-European-and-Canadian-AI-Regulation-Final-November-2021.pdf> 16, 31–32

———, 'The Rise and Fall of AI and Algorithms in American Criminal Justice: Lessons for Canada' (2020) <https://www.lco-cdo.org/wp-content/uploads/2020/10/Criminal-AI-Paper-Final-Oct-28-2020.pdf>

Lawrence, C, Cui, I and Ho, DE, 'Implementation Challenges to Three Pillars of America's AI Strategy' (2022) <https://hai.stanford.edu/white-paper-implementation-challenges-three-pillars-americas-ai-strategy> 5

Liang, PP and others, 'Towards Understanding and Mitigating Social Biases in Language Models' (2021) <http://arxiv.org/abs/2106.13219>

Liston, M, 'Administering the Canadian Rule of Law' in Colleen M Flood and Lorne Sossin (eds), *Administrative Law in Context* (Third, Emond Montgomery Publications Limited 2018) 162, 169

McFadden, M and others, 'Harmonising Artificial Intelligence: The Role of Standards in the EU AI Regulation' (2021) <https://oxcaigg.oii.ox.ac.uk/wp-content/uploads/sites/124/2021/12/Harmonising-AI-OXIL.pdf>

McGregor, L, Murray, D and Ng, V, 'International Human Rights Law as a Framework for Algorithmic Accountability' (2019) 68 International and Comparative Law Quarterly 309, 337

McLachlin, B, 'The Roles of Administrative Tribunals and Courts in Maintaining the Rule of Law' (1999) 12 *Canadian Journal of Administrative Law & Practice* 171, 174

Neapolitan, RE and Jiang, X, *Artificial Intelligence: With an Introduction to Machine Learning*, vol 1 (2nd edn, CRC Press 2018) 89–90

Obermeyer, Z and others, 'Algorithmic Bias Playbook' (2021) <https://www. chicagobooth.edu/research/center-for-applied-artificial-intelligence/research/ algorithmic-bias/playbook> 2–3

Park, A, 'Injustice Ex Machina: Predictive Algorithms in Criminal Sentencing' (2019) UCLA Law Review Law Meets World <https://www.uclalawreview.org/ injustice-ex-machina-predictive-algorithms-in-criminal-sentencing/>

Passos, IC and others, 'Machine Learning and Big Data Analytics in Bipolar Disorder: A Position Paper from the International Society for Bipolar Disorders Big Data Task Force' (2019) 21 Bipolar Disorders 582, 583

Perkowitz, S, 'The Bias in the Machine: Facial Recognition Technology and Racial Disparities' (2021) MIT Case Studies in Social and Ethical Responsibilities of Computing <https://mit-serc.pubpub.org/pub/bias-in-machine>

Phillips, PJ and others, 'National Institute of Standards and Technology Interagency or Internal Report 8312: Four Principles of Explainable Artificial Intelligence' (2020) <https://nvlpubs.nist.gov/nistpubs/ir/2020/NIST.IR.8312-draft.pdf> 4

Pottie, L and Sossin, L, 'Demystifying the Boundaries of Public Law: Policy, Discretion, and Social Welfare.' (2005) 38 UBC Law Review 147, 147, 154–155, 165–175, 179, 187

Price, PC, Jhangiani, R and Chian, I-CA, 'Reliability and Validity of Measurement' (*Research Methods in Psychology – 2nd Canadian Edition*, 2020) <https://open textbc.ca/researchmethods/chapter/reliability-and-validity-of-measurement/>

Raso, J, 'AI and Administrative Law', in Florian Martin-Bariteau and Teresa Scassa (eds), *Artificial Intelligence and the Law in Canada* (LexisNexis Canada Inc 2021) 181–182, 197

———, 'Unity in the Eye of the Beholder? Reasons for Decision in Theory and Practice in the Ontario Works Program' (2019) 70 University of Toronto Law Journal 1, 22–23

Raso, J and Scassa, T, 'Administrative Law and the Governance of Automated Decision-Making' (25 September 2020) <https://www.youtube.com/watch?v= nVs46EMAHRo>

Scassa, T, 'Administrative Law and the Governance of Automated Decision-Making' (2022) <https://www.youtube.com/watch?v=sn9AErX6ds0>

———, 'Administrative Law and the Governance of Automated Decision-Making: A Critical Look at Canada's Directive on Automated Decision-Making' (2021) 54 UBC Law Review 251, 268

Schaake, M, 'The European Commission's Artificial Intelligence Act' (2021) <https:// hai.stanford.edu/sites/default/files/2021-06/HAI_Issue-Brief_The-European-Commissions-Artificial-Intelligence-Act.pdf> 2

Schauer, FF, *Profiles, Probabilities, and Stereotypes* (Harvard University Press 2006) 3–7

Schwartz, R and others, 'A Proposal for Identifying and Managing Bias in Artificial Intelligence' (2021) <https://nvlpubs.nist.gov/nistpubs/SpecialPublications/ NIST.SP.1270-draft.pdf> 6

———, 'Towards a Standard for Identifying and Managing Bias in Artificial Intelligence' (2022) <https://nvlpubs.nist.gov/nistpubs/SpecialPublications/ NIST.SP.1270.pdf> 6–9, 15–17, 20–21, 23, 27–28, 42–43, 46, 52

Scott-Hayward, CS, *Punishing Poverty: How Bail and Pretrial Detention Fuel Inequalities in the Criminal Justice System* (University of California Press 2019) 91–92

SEBok: Guide to the Systems Engineering Body of Knowledge, 'Sociotechnical System (Glossary)' (2022) <https://www.sebokwiki.org/wiki/Sociotechnical_System_(glossary)>

Selbst, A and Barocas, S, 'The Intuitive Appeal of Explainable Machines' (2018) 87 Fordham Law Review 1085

Sharpe, RJ and Roach, K, *The Charter of Rights and Freedoms* (6th edn, Irwin Law Inc 2017) 354–406

Sheppard, C, *Inclusive Equality: The Relational Dimensions of Systemic Discrimination in Canada* (MQUP 2010) 8, 19–23, 44–46, 37–64

———, 'Of Forest Fires and Systemic Discrimination: A Review of British Columbia (Public Service Employee Relations Commission) v BCGSEU' (2001) 46 McGill Law Journal 533

Smith, D, 'An Equitable Outcome' (2020) *CBA National* <https://nationalmagazine.ca/en-ca/articles/law/in-depth/2020/an-equitable-outcome>

Sossin, L, 'Discretion Unbound: Reconciling the Charter and Soft Law' (2002) 45 Canadian Public Administration 465, 467, 480

Sossin, L and Lawrence, E, *Administrative Law in Practice: Principles and Advocacy* (Emond Publishing 2018) 27, 40–41, 124

Statistics Canada, 'Disaggregated Data Action Plan: Why It Matters to You' (2021) <https://www150.statcan.gc.ca/n1/pub/11-627-m/11-627-m2021092-eng.htm>

Supreme Court of Canada, 'Case Law in Brief: The Standard of Review (Taken from Vavilov in the "Administrative Law Trilogy")' (2019) <https://www.scc-csc.ca/case-dossier/cb/2019/37748-37896-37897-eng.pdf>

Tutt, A, 'An FDA for Algorithms' (2017) 69 Administrative Law Review 83, 107–109

UK Secretary of State for Digital Culture Media and Sport by Command of Her Majesty, 'National AI Strategy' (2021) <https://www.gov.uk/government/publications/national-ai-strategy> 40–48

Van Harten, G and others, *Administrative Law: Cases, Text, and Materials* (Seventh, Emond Montgomery Publications Limited 2015) 920–922

van Schendel, S, 'The Challenges of Risk Profiling Used by Law Enforcement: Examining the Cases of COMPAS and SyRI' in Leonie Reins (ed), *Regulating New Technologies in Uncertain Times* (Springer-Verlag Berlin Heidelberg 2019)

Veale, M and Borgesius, FZ, 'Demystifying the Draft EU Artificial Intelligence Act — Analysing the Good, the Bad, and the Unclear Elements of the Proposed Approach' (2021) 22 Computer Law Review International 97, 105–106

Vizkelety, B, *Proving Discrimination in Canada* (Carswell 1987) 133–192

Wachter, S and Mittelstadt, B, 'A Right to Reasonable Inferences: Re-Thinking Data Protection Law in the Age of Big Data and AI' (2019) Columbia Business Law Review 494, 501, 575, 585, 587

Webb, GI and others, 'Characterizing Concept Drift' (2016) 30 Data Mining and Knowledge Discovery 964 <http://link.springer.com/10.1007/s10618-015-0448-4>

Werder, K, Ramesh, B and Zhang, R (Sophia), 'Establishing Data Provenance for Responsible Artificial Intelligence Systems' (2022) 13 ACM Transactions on Management Information Systems 1 <https://dl.acm.org/doi/10.1145/3503488>

West, DM and Allen, JR, *Turning Point: Policymaking in the Era of Artificial Intelligence* (Brookings Institution Press 2020)

Wildeman, S, 'Making Sense of Reasonableness' in Colleen M Flood and Lorne Sossin (eds), *Administrative Law in Context* (Third, Emond Montgomery Publications Limited 2018) 463, 499–504

Winfield, AFT and others, 'IEEE P7001: A Proposed Standard on Transparency' (2021) 8 Frontiers in Robotics and AI <https://www.frontiersin.org/articles/10.3389/frobt.2021.665729/full>

Xiang, A, 'Reconciling Legal and Technical Approaches to Algorithmic Bias' (2021) 88 Tennessee Law Review 649, 666–674, 705–723

Zhou, X and others, 'A Framework to Monitor Machine Learning Systems Using Concept Drift Detection' in Witold Abramowicz and Rafael Corchuelo (eds), *Lecture Notes in Business Information Processing* (22nd Inter, 2019) <http://link.springer.com/10.1007/978-3-030-20485-3_17>

CANADIAN LEGAL CASES

Andrews v Law Society of British Columbia [1989] 1 SCR 143

Auton (Guardian ad litem of) v British Columbia (Attorney General) (2004) SCC 78

Baker v Minister of Citizenship and Immigration [1999] 2 SCR 817

Cardinal v. Director of Kent Institution [1985] 2 SCR 643

Doré v Barreau du Québec [2012] 1 SCR 395

Dunsmuir v New Brunswick [2008] 1 SCR 190

Edmonton (City) v. Edmonton East (Capilano) Shopping Centres Ltd [2016] 2 SCR 293

Fraser v Canada (Attorney General) [2020] SCC 28

R. v. Kapp [2008] 2 SCR 483

US LEGAL CASES

State v Loomis 881 N.W.2d 749 (Wis 2016)

CANADIAN LEGISLATION

Bill C-27: An Act to enact the Consumer Privacy Protection Act, the Personal Information and Data Protection Tribunal Act and the Artificial Intelligence and Data Act and to make consequential and related amendments to other Acts, 44th Parliament, 1st session (2022) <https://www.parl.ca/legisinfo/en/bill/44-1/c-27?view=details#bill-profile-tabs> (proposed)

Bill 64: An Act to modernize legislative provisions as regards the protection of personal information (2021) <https://www.assnat.qc.ca/en/travaux-parlementaires/projets-loi/projet-loi-64-42-1.html>

Constitution Act, 1982 <https://laws-lois.justice.gc.ca/eng/const/page-12.html#h-39>

Employment Equity Act S.C., 1995, c. 44 <https://laws-lois.justice.gc.ca/eng/acts/e-5.401/page-1.html>

Privacy Act R.S.C., 1985, c. P-21 <https://laws-lois.justice.gc.ca/eng/acts/p-21/fulltext.html#:~:text=Purpose%20of%20Act&text=2%20The%20purpose%20of%20this,of%20access%20to%20that%20information.>

LEGISLATION (OTHER JURISDICTIONS)

European Commission, 'Draft Standardisation Request to the European Standardisation Organisations in Support of Safe and Trustworthy Artificial Intelligence' (2022) <https://ec.europa.eu/docsroom/documents/52376> (proposed)

————, 'Proposal for a Regulation of the European Parliament and of the Council Laying Down Harmonised Rules on Artificial Intelligence (Artificial Intelligence Act) and Amending Certain Union Legislative Acts' (2021) <https://digital-strategy.ec.europa.eu/en/library/proposal-regulation-european-approach-artificial-intelligence> (proposed)

Equal Employment Opportunity Commission Information on Impact 1978 29 CFR § 1607.4 (1978) <https://www.govinfo.gov/app/details/CFR-2014-title29-vol4/CFR-2014-title29-vol4-sec1607-4>

Regulation (EU) 2016/679 of the European Parliament and of the Council (General Data Protection Regulation) (2016) <https://gdpr-info.eu/>

Index

Note: Page numbers in **bold** indicate tables and those with "n" indicate footnotes.

For Product Safety Concerns and Information please contact our EU
representative GPSR@taylorandfrancis.com
Taylor & Francis Verlag GmbH, Kaufingerstraße 24, 80331 München, Germany

www.ingramcontent.com/pod-product-compliance
Lightning Source LLC
Chambersburg PA
CBHW050719280326
41926CB00088B/3286